P9-ELX-841

LOVE & JUSTICE

LOVE & JUSTICE

A Journey of Empowerment, Activism, and Embracing Black Beauty

Laetitia Ky

Princeton Architectural Press, New York

Contents

INTRODUCTION

My awareness of both love and justice began in what might seem like an unlikely place: the world of beauty and fashion.

I started experimenting with hair braiding when I was five years old. Growing up, I loved playing with dolls and Barbies. But because there are no doll companies in Ivory Coast—almost all toys are imported—I had only White Barbies, with hair unlike mine. I couldn't braid their hair because it was so straight and slippery.

To solve that problem, I bought adult curly hair extensions, cut all my Barbies' hair off, and then implanted the curly extensions into their heads with a needle and thread! (It certainly strikes me as symbolic that while lots of little girls chop off the hair of their Barbie dolls and leave it at that, I opted to literally sew in new hair instead!) I was very meticulous—it had to be done. I must have improved more than twenty dolls!

My adventures with hair didn't end there. I started creating hair sculptures about five years ago, during a period when I was attempting to reconcile myself with my African heritage. As in many parts of the world, urban society and culture in Ivory Coast has been largely Westernized. Most of my beauty and fashion references growing up—through toys, TV, and other forms of media—were entirely influenced by Western culture. Of course, a few characters on television and in film, pop culture figures, and fashion standards were specific to us, but there weren't enough to provide positive models of what it means to be African.

Beauty has always been both a passion and a personal struggle for me. Only when I started to love myself as a dark-skinned African woman did I begin to learn more about my culture. Doing so was a radical act, given how embedded White/Western supremacy is in African culture. I researched different African tribes—how they dressed, how they styled their hair, how they wore their makeup, and their aesthetics in general. I wanted to incorporate more traditional African beauty into my own style to express my pride.

I created my Instagram account in 2015, and began posting my hair sculptures in 2017. In the early days, I made my hair sculptures mostly for my own enjoyment—to express my passion for art and beauty with the people around me. I had been sharing my work steadily on Instagram for a couple of years when a photo series I posted went viral. I had shaped my hair into a pair of hands, and those hands were performing different actions in each photo. There were twelve pictures in that series, and all of them were shared and reposted across the world; the photo that was most widely shared was one in which my hair hands were holding my glasses, while my real hands were holding a book.

In a two-week period, my Instagram account went from 4,000 to 30,000 followers. Several people who reposted my art expressed their amazement. I received messages from people who gushed that they'd never seen anything like that before. Some loved it because it was fun; others loved it because using Black hair to create art made a powerful and original statement. Many people even thought my images were Photoshopped until I began posting videos of myself creating my hair art.

In addition to feeling surprised at gaining so many followers, I was especially gratified by the people who thanked me because my work helped them love themselves a little more. Back when my posts only reached my friends and family, their reactions were positive and encouraging enough, but no one had ever indicated that my art had helped them or transformed the way they viewed themselves or thought about beauty.

The more I posted photos of myself and my art on Instagram, the more messages I received from people telling me they were inspired by what I was doing, and by the way I was highlighting my natural hair. I was surprised to see that my work could have this much of an impact. It was a turning point for me. After that, simply creating cute and fun images wasn't enough. I knew I had to use this new power to spread strong messages that would address topics that were important to me. I wanted to be something so much more than a beautiful face. I wanted to be a force of transformation.

To give you a sense of why I felt so strongly about using my voice and platform to spread awareness...to be a voice that amplifies themes of unequivocal self-love, social transformation, and justice...it's important to tell you about my journey.

For lots of people today, Instagram fame is the gateway to success. Having hundreds of thousands to millions of followers can be seen as a sign that you've made it in the world, that you have the kind of social capital to do whatever you want.

That certainly wasn't the case for me.

My beginnings in the world of social media influencing and model-ing weren't easy. While I had amassed a large number of followers and was collaborating with a few brands, I certainly wasn't paying the bills with my hair art. My Instagram wasn't a full-time job, by any means, but I knew I was onto something big. However, many brands that reached out to me in the early days wanted to give me a free product in exchange for the promotion, rather than financially compensate me for my work. I'm happy to say I always turned down those offers; it seemed obvious they didn't value the art enough. And artists—especially Black women artists, whose ideas may be circulated widely but not compensated fairly—deserve to be paid.

When I decided that I wanted to live and work in the art and entertainment industry, friends and even some family members thought I was crazy. They said I was too intelligent to choose such a path, that I had the potential to be brilliant in another field. They told me over and over again that Ivory Coast isn't a country where an artist can live decently. I replied that I didn't want to work only in Ivory Coast, but all over the world. To them, this was unrealistically optimistic.

After three years of college, I stopped my studies and spent a whole year thinking about what to do next. All I had was a phone, the Internet, and my own creativity. When I decided to use those three tools to open doors, I experienced many ups and downs. Even as I was gaining a lot of exposure on Instagram—even if my posts were liked thousands of times—real, paid opportunities that would enable me to launch a career as an artist were still scarce.

I have always dreamed of becoming an actress, and when I was looking for ways to pay for acting classes, I started to consider modeling. But I've never viewed modeling as simply a stepping stone to something else—it is also something I love, something that enables me to express parts of myself and my identity that might otherwise remain hidden.

A little over a year ago, I decided to do everything I could to be signed by an agency, which is when I discovered how hard it is to break into the modeling industry. I researched the biggest agencies in the world, then I took a lot of Polaroids—simple, basic pictures that models take without makeup to show their features—with the help of my little sister, and I sent out those pictures. I also used specific hashtags for my posts on Instagram that young models use when they wish to be scouted. I ran into my first obstacle when I realized that many agencies' minimum height is 5'9"—I'm 5'8". In addition, the maximum age for women was twenty-four; I was almost twenty-three. I realized that if I wasn't scouted that year, I might have to give up just as I was getting started.

I was thrilled to receive inquiries from several big agencies in the United States, but in the end, each turned me down for one reason or another (my height, my age, my location, or the fact that I couldn't attend open calls). I was always looking on the Internet for famous and successful models who were under 5'8" to encourage and motivate myself, but there weren't many of them. And forget about "short" Black supermodels—they were practically nonexistent. It was a depressing realization.

With all of these factors working against me, I became convinced that I needed to come up with a new life plan entirely. I stopped sending emails and using Instagram hashtags and started to think about other ways to pay for acting classes, even as I continued to post my art regularly. Then one day, a few months after I'd given up, I received a DM from Elite Model Management that changed my life. What's funny is that when I was applying to all the big agencies, I'd skipped Elite because I'd noticed that the models they worked with were generally very tall, so I didn't imagine they would ever be interested in me.

I was about to pick my sister up from school when my phone buzzed. When I opened the message and saw it was from someone at Elite, I froze. It took me a few minutes to realize I was being given another chance to do what I dreamed of doing. The person followed up by telling me they were impressed with my profile and wanted me to be a contestant in Elite Model Look's brand-new Influencer category for their 2019 modeling competition. I had never been so excited, and everyone at home was thrilled for me. I told my mom, who was about to borrow money to pay for my acting classes, to hold off—because if I won, we wouldn't have to borrow anything!

A few months later, I went to Paris for the competition. I was up against six other people in my category, and each of them had their own specialty as an influencer. Despite all my doubts, I won the contest! I had been full of dreams and ideas for projects without knowing how I would accomplish them, or even what steps to take in the direction of my new life. I had been afraid that all of those people I knew who'd told me to give up were right. Winning the contest meant everything to me because it symbolized something important: it was the first time I really felt that all the hard work, all the hours I'd spent on my art, was paying off.

I started working out the details with my Elite team about my move to New York. Unfortunately, the global pandemic put everything on hold. However, even from Ivory Coast, I've been able to work with a few brands and build my knowledge of the industry.

For the moment, though, the most powerful change of all has been my mindset. I'm more hopeful and enthusiastic about my future, and the doubts have almost vanished. (I say "almost," because everyone has experiences in which their confidence takes a temporary beating!)

I know that after this crisis is over, I'll have the opportunities I need to build a future for myself. I've also gained a new level of credibility since signing with Elite. Today, brands and individuals don't request that I promote them on my Instagram feed in exchange for just a free product. My image is tied to my art—and both speak loudly and clearly to the fact that I have something powerful to say that is worth taking note of... and taking seriously!

Why am I sharing all of this? Because I know from firsthand experience that dreams come true, no matter who you are or where in the world you might be. Our societies and cultures across the globe are rapidly changing. Everything from the awareness of false standards of beauty and worth to grassroots movements like Black Lives Matter is transforming the stereotypes and prejudices

we hold about whose stories count. Thanks to the growing possibilities offered by social media, the range of who and what is being represented in the art world and media is expanding, especially as artists and activists like me are becoming more vocal about our experiences.

Those of us who have been historically invisible are rising up to share our wisdom and our beauty with the world.

For me, this is all a beginning. I'm interested in having a career beyond acting and modeling, and I hope to move my art beyond social media into the physical gallery world. As my experiences and artistic knowledge evolve, I am willing to accept any opportunity that feels right to me, and the path that I'm currently on feels more than right.

My art is inspired by elements in the world around me: politics, social movements, feminism, body positivity, natural beauty, African aesthetics, random images and sound, my feelings, and so much more. With this book, I hope to show the world, especially young women, that anything is possible with hard work, fierce determination, and passion for what you do. The capacity to speak out and take ownership of your voice and your image is empowering in and of itself, and it also enables you to advocate for others who may not have the same luxury. The power of women's voices and ideas—and our unique beauty—is transforming oppressive social norms. In celebrating our beauty, we are fierce champions of a more inclusive and equitable world.

I know my activist art stands out because the messages I send are delivered in an unusual way. If you can find a unique way to speak about a subject, you can influence people who otherwise might have ignored it. It's all about starting from exactly where you are and accepting "your one wild and precious life"—as the poet Mary Oliver described it. That is the best path I can think of toward love and justice.

1

CELEBRATING MY AFRICAN HERITAGE

My Childhood in Ivory Coast

I was born and grew up in Ivory Coast, a diverse West African country that is full of warmth and joy, and that made me the person I am today. I had a happy childhood, full of long hours spent playing BICICI (the Ivorian equivalent of Chinese jump rope), singing, dancing in the sand with my friends, and eating delicious *gbofloto* (a donut-like delicacy that is also known as *puff puff, mitake,* or *botokoin,* depending on the country) every morning on my way to school.

I soaked in the infinite love and joy all around me. I have many beautiful memories of my childhood: eating my delicious millet porridge every morning...playing with my friends in the sand and rocks every afternoon...singing and dancing beneath the warm rain...relishing the feeling of complete freedom that seemed so easily within reach.

In contrast to these happy memories are painful moments of discrimination and alienation that I felt as a dark-skinned child, not to mention the sexism I experienced as a young girl. Despite Ivorians' notions of our country's modernization and progress, our society is still deeply impacted by the traces of French colonization. There is a pattern of collective trauma that is still evident today; Ivorians' self-esteem has been weakened by years of conditioning based on the internalized belief that being Black and African is inferior.

The Inferiority Complex

Ivorian society has its own specific codes and cultural legacies, but our relationship to our traditions continues to transform, especially in the aftermath of colonialism and under the effects of globalization. While many people speak of the progress that has graced our society due to these outside influences, fewer talk about the deeply instilled inferiority complex that has informed Africans' ideas about who we are.

Our skin, our hair, and our culture have been devalued to such an extent that despite the movement toward African pride and reclamation of who we are, we still unconsciously believe we are not enough. We constantly try to emulate Western culture, aesthetics, lifestyles, and trends. Most of the beauty and fashion references I had growing up were entirely influenced by Western culture. At school, we learned more about Western history than our own! Even though certain characters on television and in film, as well as pop culture icons and fashion standards, were particular to our own traditions and histories, they weren't enough to teach me what it means to be African. I had to come to that understanding on my own.

There is a great deal of pressure to imitate Europeans, in everything from language to clothing to education to the ways we design our societies. If we don't do this, we don't feel "civilized" enough. In and out of Africa, there is an unspoken belief that "European" denotes high class, whereas "African" indicates all things low class, savage, and archaic. This is embedded in everything: how we do our hair or perceive our skin, as well as the ways we eat, talk, and dress. No matter our class or social position, there is a constant pressure to change our behavior and our looks to appear more European than African. The perception is that the more light-skinned you are, the more beautiful you look, and that the more straight and silky your hair is, the more European your appearance, and therefore, the more distinguished and worthy you are.

Africa is a continent with a rich history—including glorious accomplishments and innovations. Sadly, our history also reflects the harmful effects of colonialism on all fifty-four of Africa's present-day countries; these effects are felt today on many levels, both obvious and not so obvious.

The people we are taught to look up to, such as teachers and other educated people, may inadvertently perpetuate the stereotypes and beliefs that maintain this collective inferiority complex and the idea that "Black" is inherently bad or evil. Without our conscious awareness, we are often indirectly taught to hate the very things that make us beautiful and unique. This miseducation has far-reaching consequences for our connection to our past, our present, and our future.

Even as we Africans do our very best to restore a sense of beauty and accomplishment to our continent—by returning to the very best parts of our culture, promoting them, and making them visible—the road to true independence remains long. But little by little, Africa's people are building our future by drawing inspiration and strength from the culture and habits our colonizers tried, and failed, to erase.

Our Disappearing Culture and Lifestyle

The African inferiority complex extends beyond how we view ourselves physically and touches how we live. Sadly, African spirituality is generally derided as "demonic" or "witchcraft." While traditional African religions are still practiced, this occurs with great secrecy. Only the religions that came with colonization are accepted today, and anyone who uses traditional medicine instead of "modern" Western medicine is perceived as crazy and irresponsible.

Unfortunately, the mother tongue (and there are more than sixty mother tongues in Ivory Coast) is not widely perceived as important or a source of national pride. Speaking it simply means that one is a "villager," whereas being able to express oneself in French establishes a person as being educated. And if a person talks without an Ivorian accent, they are viewed as proper and eloquent for speaking like a White person. Even if your syntax and vocabulary are perfect, having an Ivorian accent that is too strong means you are "low class."

Although Ivorians have gorgeous traditional fabrics that can be used to create stunning garments, it's rare to see people reveling in the beauty of our textiles. Many people prefer to wear Western-style clothing at work, at home, and for big occasions.

If you love to eat Ivorian food, you are not viewed as refined. Some people even brag when they eat things like pizza and burgers instead of traditional Ivorian soups and other dishes. The preference for Western food, even fast food, signifies that you have money. I used to lie when people would ask me what I liked to eat, since it was embarrassing to admit that I loved *foutou*, *gombo*, and other traditional Ivorian dishes.

The traditional cuisines of Africa are based around fruits, vegetables, and grains and also include dairy products and meat. These dishes are composed of locally available ingredients and do not usually include nonnative, imported foods.

The great variety of recipes and ways of eating are dependent on each country and its customs. In Ivory Coast, one of my favorite meals is called *foutou*. It is a mix of plantains and cassava that have been boiled, pounded, and formed into balls. You can eat the dish with a variety of local soups (groundnut, gombo, palm soup, etc.). The process of making foutou is arduous—you need lots of strength to manually grind the ingredients using a mortar and pestle.

The art of African mask making can be traced back to well before Paleolithic times. These artworks were traditionally (and still are) made of a variety of materials, including leather, metal, fabric, and different types of wood. Masks have played an important role in certain forms of African art and spirituality. They serve as ritual objects with many purposes, such as ensuring a good harvest, addressing tribal needs in times of peace or war, or conveying the presence of gods or deceased ancestors in initiation rituals or burial ceremonies. Sometimes, they symbolize totem animals or creatures with special significance.

Head carrying is popular in Ivory Coast and throughout Africa. It's common to see women carrying pots of cloth shaped into a ring or ball, as well as fruits and vegetables, wood, water, and just about anything else you can imagine. A study from Nairobi demonstrated that African women can carry up to 20 percent of their weight on their head without increasing their rate of energy consumption, simply because it is such an ingrained cultural habit!

Music is an integral part of African culture. African music is traditionally played at gatherings on special occasions. The traditional music of Africa is ancient, rich, and—given the vastness of the continent—diverse.

The *djembe* and the *kora* are two of my favorite instruments. A djembe is a West African hand drum, traditionally carved from a single piece of wood and covered in animal skin. The name *djembe* is said to come from the Bambara people of Mali, whose expression "*Anke djé, anke bé*" translates to "Everyone, gather together in peace." When I was in elementary school and took music classes, I always picked the djembe—I loved how easy it was to create a rhythm!

The kora is a string instrument used extensively in West Africa. A kora typically has twenty-one strings, which are plucked with the fingers. It combines features of the lute and the harp. I love how it sounds; some of my favorite memories of the kora are when my mother played music by Salif Keita, a famous Malian singer whose songs often include the instrument.

Sacred Connections to Wildlife

Just as family is a great source of pride in Africa, so is our connection to the land and to our nonhuman family. For hundreds of years, Africans have held a deep reverence for the animals we are surrounded by, a relationship amplified by our reliance on them for food, clothing, and artistic inspiration. Customs vary from tribe to tribe, but all maintain the idea of balance and equality between human and animal, as well as the importance of refraining from unnecessary killing.

Africans place great symbolic significance on the animals around us; each animal carries its own unique meaning, spirit, and power. Animals can be considered totems—symbolic guides and spirit helpers or allies that enable us to make meaning of our own lives and of the worlds beyond this reality.

The Effects of Racial Privilege

The way we treat White people in Ivory Coast reveals the complexity of our ingrained cultural beliefs. In some schools, such as the one I attended, most girls are forced to cut their hair because it's supposed to help them focus on education instead of beauty, but White girls are allowed to keep their hair long.

When I was a child, maybe around six or seven years old, I went to a supermarket with my dad. I noticed a little White girl who was with her mom. She was eating ice cream, and when she finished, she threw the ice-cream paper on the floor. The woman who was cleaning the supermarket quickly took the paper and put it in the trash can without saying anything to the little girl. I had something in my hand that I too threw onto the floor. I didn't realize it was rude to do that; seeing the White girl do it without consequences made me think it was OK. But as soon as I threw my paper, the same lady who didn't say a thing just a moment before yelled violently at me and ordered me to pick up my garbage. I did so, but I was shocked at the difference in her reaction.

Over the years, I have experienced other similar things, such as ordering a coffee before a White person but receiving mine after theirs. I have recognized this tendency to treat White people with more kindness, patience, and respect than fellow Black Ivorian people. Even in the corporate world, a White person may be paid more money for a position than a Black one with similar experience.

The continued privilege of White people, even as a minority, highlights the ways in which the inferiority complex is so deeply embedded in our culture. I know that many Africans, and even White people, are seeking to be forces of change, especially as the world evolves in its understanding of racial injustice. At the same time, change can be a slow process that requires patience, education, and persistence.

Beauty and Skin Color

Skin color is a powerful aspect of Ivorian identity that's embedded in our unspoken inferiority complex. In the aftermath of colonization, which taught us that dark skin is less beautiful than pale skin, many people still walk around with the belief that they are ugly.

During colonization, some people with lighter skin had access to opportunities that were usually only afforded to White people. In our current society, this flawed favoritism hasn't changed much. The lighter you are, the more beautiful you are considered—and we all know that we live in a world where being beautiful can amplify our chances of being successful.

I'd never thought much about my skin color until the age of ten, when kids at school gave me a pejorative nickname related to the darkness of my skin. I was troubled, but it wasn't a fixation at first. Over time, very slowly, I started to wish my skin was lighter. I even remember asking my mom for permission to bleach my skin. Skin bleaching entails using products that lighten dark areas on the skin to attain a lighter complexion. These products are extremely popular across Africa and in other parts of the world (many of which have populations with naturally dark skin) and include creams, soaps, and professional treatments.

My mother replied with a big no. She said that I couldn't make this decision at such a young age, but that once I turned eighteen I would have the right to do so. I was so mad, because some girls my age who went to my school had already started bleaching their skin. A lot of the other women around me were also doing the same.

I remember a nice woman who worked in our home; she slept in my bedroom because we didn't have a separate room available. As much as I loved and appreciated this woman, it was terrible to share a room with her, as her nightly ritual was to apply bleaching cream just before bed and it had a disgusting smell that made me want to vomit. I recall waiting in the living room every night because it would take at least two hours for the stench to dissipate. I was too shy to ask her to stop using the offending product, so I endured the torture.

Most of the skin-bleaching products in Africa are inexpensive and have an awful smell; the full ingredients are usually not listed, so people don't even know what they are putting on their skin. Vendors with no expertise in chemistry create weird concoctions with potentially harmful ingredients to help women lighten their skin

TOO BLACK

quickly. Some of the products are reputed to make you "White" in three days. Most women are aware of the dangers of putting these toxic preparations on their skin, but having light skin is their highest priority.

I assumed that the smell of my roommate's product indicated it was of poor quality, and honestly, the results on her skin weren't any better. She had become very light-skinned, but she had uneven patches all over her body. Some parts of her face, hands, and legs were extremely black. The contrast between her overall light skin and the dark patches on her face and body made her look almost as if she'd been burned. Her skin was also covered in angry red pimples and looked very unhealthy, but she seemed to feel that the light skin was worth all the drawbacks.

One of my aunts also used to bleach her skin; while her products were of higher quality, she still experienced side effects. Once, when she needed surgery, it didn't go well, as her skin was so weak that the doctors couldn't sew it together afterward. Sadly, she was close to death, and her recovery was long.

Seeing all of this, and even more, didn't discourage me. I still wanted to bleach my skin, telling myself I would use only the highest-quality products. The cautionary stories all around me hadn't done anything to alleviate the pain of feeling "less than"; I remember being extremely jealous every time I saw mixed-race women who had lighter skin than I did. I wanted all the attention people gave them. I wanted to be considered just as beautiful and just as deserving of respect. I constantly asked the universe why it had decided to curse me with dark skin while gracing other women with pretty, fair skin.

When I think about how I feel today versus how I felt at that time, the contrast is stark. I have grown so much in my self-acceptance. Today, my dark skin is one of the features I most appreciate about myself. Knowing this helps me see that when people feel insecure, often the real problem isn't something about their bodies but something that is deeply embedded in their minds.

My Hair and Me

My relationship with my hair has evolved a lot over the years. I don't have any memories of being a child with natural hair. My hair was relaxed for the first time when I was five years old. (The relaxing procedure uses chemicals that straighten the hair by breaking down and reformulating the hair's components. By relaxing the hair, you can soften tight or kinky curls.)

Throughout my childhood, my hair was relaxed every three months. My hair was naturally long and strong, but from the ages of nine to twelve, I was forced to shave it all off in an effort to help me focus on my education. It was assumed that "beautiful" girls with long hair would spend too much time caring for their hair and would focus on boys and dating instead of their studies. At school, if we forgot to shave our heads, we weren't allowed to go into class; sometimes they'd even dole out humiliating punishments like cutting and disfiguring our hair with scissors in front of the entire class. I hated it. I was in love with my hair, and it was an important part of my identity and self-expression, so this time was very difficult for me.

When I turned thirteen, I was no longer forced to observe this rule. I was ready to enjoy my hair once more and let it grow back. Because I was older, I was no longer interested in the cute, childish braids that I was accustomed to years before; instead I gravitated toward hairstyles that required my hair to be perfectly straight. I had no idea how to properly care for my hair. I relaxed my hair once a month, sometimes even every three weeks. On top of the pain and discomfort of the relaxation process, I chose hairstyles that were extremely stressful for my hair and scalp. My routine consisted of relaxing my hair, dyeing it, washing it, putting in some weave, or locking it into a tight braid. By the time I was fifteen years old, my hair was weak, thin, brittle, and extremely damaged.

I didn't question any of it, because relaxing and straightening our hair was the norm. I had only ever known my hair as being straight, and absolutely everyone around me had relaxed hair, too. Our hair was considered ugly if we left too much time between relaxing sessions, as the natural root underneath the straight ends made a person look strange. This meant that as soon as our natural hair became noticeable, we had to relax it again.

To be honest, I didn't even know that wearing my natural hair was an option. I didn't have any role models to show me this was possible. Even the dolls I had as a child were all White, with

straight hair. I was fine with it; I didn't ask myself too many questions about the *why* of hair relaxation. I simply thought to myself: *Not everyone can have the long, straight hair of my Barbie dolls or of the White people on TV and in movies. At least relaxer exists, so we can all look a little more beautiful.*

One day, I saw a picture of Beyoncé with some beautiful braids, and I decided to try the same hairstyle. I brought the picture to a hair salon; after five hours of braiding, my hair looked beautiful like hers, even though the braids were extremely tight and uncomfortable. But at that time, tightness was seen as an indication of good braiding, and trading my comfort for beauty was normal to me.

It was always hard to sleep for the first three or four days after braiding my hair. I didn't mind, but as the days passed, I noticed that the hair toward the front of my head was falling out. Over time, some of the small braids toward the front of my head also began to fall out.

Normally, I would keep a hairstyle for at least three weeks, but because of what was happening, I undid the braids after ten days—and it was a disaster. As I brushed my hair, it seemed as if I had lost a quarter of it. I shed lots of tears that day for my lost hair, which was a huge shock to me. Even though I knew my hair had become damaged due to improper care, I'd never lost this much hair because of a single hairstyle!

The next hairstyle I received was a weave with bangs to hide my hair loss. I kept it for a month, and when I took it out, my hair looked even worse. I began looking for solutions on the Internet and YouTube to make my hair grow back—and I discovered the Black American natural hair community. I was in awe! At fifteen years old, I was seeing for the very first time that not only was it a viable option to refrain from relaxing my hair—but also, it was possible for people who look like me to be beautiful wearing their natural hair. I discovered tips and tricks for proper hair care, and I quickly came to realize that my hair routine was bad not only for my hair but also for my entire health. It was a major turning point that would open a path to new possibilities around beauty, pride, and self-esteem.

Learning to Love My Roots

Reconciling with my African heritage started with my discovery of the African American natural hair community. I was enthralled by all the beautiful Black women on YouTube proudly rocking their natural hair and sharing ways to take care of it. I could have watched these women doing their hair for hours and hours! I had been so conditioned by my environment to relax my hair that it had become as essential as wearing clothes, brushing my teeth, or eating. I couldn't imagine being happy with a head full of the new growth that was painful to comb if I went a month without relaxer.

Needless to say, discovering the natural hair community was an epiphany. I became deeply introspective about what it meant to have grown up in a world where all of us believed we needed to make a tremendous effort to be enough and to be seen as beautiful. I was so inspired that I decided to shave my head entirely to embrace what the universe had given me. My mom, sisters, and friends didn't understand my radical shift. My mom thought it was a bad idea because I would lose my relatively long hair without even being sure I would enjoy having natural hair. But she was very supportive and sent me to a hairdresser. It was an emotional moment. As they shaved my head, I cried. What I felt was a mixture of fear and excitement. On the one hand, I was afraid to face who I really was, but I was also exhilarated at the idea of not having to hide my true self anymore.

When it was over, they asked me if I wanted to keep the hair they'd cut. I said no. I was ready to let go of the years of insecurity that my old hair symbolized.

Despite my initial optimism, coming back to my natural hair was extremely hard. The first months were easy because my hair was short. I loved the feeling of my closely cropped 4C coils. My hair wasn't soft at all, but it was *mine*. After the fifth month, however, things became challenging as my hair grew longer and required more maintenance. No product was good enough to make my hair soft and easy to comb. The advice on YouTube didn't help, either: most of the women doing these tutorials had naturally curly hair instead of coils like mine, so the techniques they used didn't work for me, and the products they were advising newly natural girls like me to use were available in the United States but not in Ivory Coast.

There were moments when my scalp hurt so much from combing my hair that I cried. Sometimes, I even experienced a sense of vague regret for my decision to go natural—a feeling I quickly turned away. Today, I'm so happy I didn't go back to relaxing my hair, even when my decision felt hard. Of course, I made so many mistakes with my natural hair in the beginning that I had to do another big chop after a year. Braids, weaves, and wigs helped me a lot during that phase—this time, I wasn't using those styles to hide my hair but to protect it. Wearing protective styles helped me to avoid unnecessarily stressing my hair, as Type 4C hair, the most densely packed and tightly coiled, tends to be more delicate than other hair types and doesn't require daily combing and manipulation.

I continued to learn about my hair, and over time, it felt better. In 2016, my favorite protective style became Havana twists—twists made with kinky hair extensions that look like real 4C hair. In addition to being pretty, they are easy to moisturize and wash. Also, when I used regular braid extensions, you could easily see the difference in texture between my hair and the extensions after just a week. With kinky extensions, I didn't have that problem.

The more time that passed, the more I chose protective styles that look like natural hair, because I was starting to appreciate everything associated with being Black. Instead of choosing straight, wavy, or curly hair extensions, I selected the coiliest Afro textures I could find. I had once rejected my natural hair, but I now gravitated toward kinkiness and all its textured glory.

Learning to love my hair naturally helped me to love and appreciate my other Black features, including my beautiful dark skin and my face with its big nose. Falling in love with my hair made me fall in love with my Blackness. I began to appreciate the African aesthetic, with its vibrant hairstyles, clothes, and colors. In this period, I pierced my septum—a trend that is currently popular but is inspired by the traditional style of Fulani women, an ethnic group in West Africa. My preferred clothing and jewelry had a distinctly African flair, and these new styles became a way of expressing my pride in my origins and my inner self.

Looking for inspiration, I started to follow a lot of Afrocentric pages on Facebook and Instagram. One day, while scrolling through social media, I came across a photo album of traditional hairstyles worn by African women in the early twentieth century. The hairstyles were impressive, beautiful, and uniquely Black. They made me want to experiment with my own kinky braids, which I was now wearing every day.

These portraits of African women with beautiful hairstyles were taken by Christian missionaries in the early twentieth century. There are records of each photo's location and time period, but the women's names are unknown.

Top left and right: Wangara woman, 1928–1936
Bottom left: Women in Zanzibar, 1908–1912
Bottom right: Woman in Congo, 1920–1940

Top left: Mangbetu woman, 1920–1940
Top right: Southern African woman, date unknown
Bottom: Women in Ghana, 1885–1908

This is how I started the art of sculpting with my hair. For my first sculpture, I attempted to make my hair stand high. When I saw it was possible, I instantly took a photo and posted it on Facebook—all my friends were amazed. The reactions were so positive that I started posting more and more photos of new and exciting styles that revealed the range of possibilities. Each photo I posted got more likes, comments, and shares than the previous one.

The encouragement kept me going.

I am touched by all the comments from Black women who have informed me that they used to hate their hair, but that seeing my work has instilled in them a new appreciation for their features. Once, a woman told me she convinced her five-year-old daughter not to ask for straight hair after she showed the child my photos. This touched my heart. Another Ivorian woman also told me she stopped using skin-bleaching products because I was the first person to show her how beautiful dark skin can be. Many artists have said that I've given them the motivation to express themselves wholeheartedly, even when they are unsure of how others will respond or even if people will like their art.

I've learned that by choosing not to relax my hair, I am reclaiming my heritage—and that in unabashedly being myself, I'm giving others space to be true to themselves and to recognize and celebrate their own unique beauty.

Black Hair Is Beautiful

Hair played a major cultural function in precolonial societies. Depending on the society, African people used hairstyles to communicate their religion, wealth, age, social class, tribe, ethnic affiliation, and marital status, among other important factors of their identity.

Hair also displayed information about fertility and vitality—the more hair someone had, the more fertile, strong, healthy, and powerful they were perceived to be. In addition, it had spiritual connotations, as hair was believed to be a way to communicate with the divine. The longer a person's hair, the more receptive they were thought to be to messages from deities and other spirit entities.

People didn't go to hairstylists; hairdressing was left in the hands of trusted friends and relatives. Because of the strong relationship between one's hair and spiritual power, the danger of leaving one's hair in the hands of enemies was omnipresent. It was believed that hair could be used to produce a "charm" to injure its owner.

Over the centuries, Africans have generated a variety of creative hairstyles—not only tresses, cornrows, and braided styles but also ornamental styles that include beads, gold, and cowrie shells. While many of these styles disappeared from the continent in the wake of colonization, we are beginning to see a revival of appreciation for the diversity, creativity, and beauty of African hair.

During slavery, African hair was called "woolly," likening Black people to animals. It was referred to as "ugly" and "unwanted"; those words and others dehumanized enslaved people. This trauma and self-hatred has been passed down for generations and continues to this day; hair straightening and relaxing is just a byproduct of it.

Going natural has helped me reclaim not only my heritage but also my humanity, my worth, and my beauty. And it is my hope that the hairstyles that helped to define my continent will make a reappearance in the world, birth even more looks, and open people's eyes to the beauty of Black hair.

Family: My Blood, My Love

Family has traditionally played a central role in African societies, and Ivory Coast is no exception. Many households include not only the nuclear family but also the extended family. Retirement homes don't even exist here, as caring for family is such an important value in African culture.

However, since I was young, I've always lived far from my extended family. It isn't that I don't see my cousins, grandparents, aunts, and uncles, but those interactions have been rare. I grew up around my dad, mom, and little sister until my parents' divorce, which left me with only my mother and sister—the two most important people in my life. Both of them

African mothers often carry their babies on their backs. It reinforces the bond between a mother and her child; the baby is always close to the mother during the day, either awake or asleep, accompanying her during her various errands and chores. My mom used to carry me this way to help me sleep. She did the same for my little sister.

shaped the person I am today, and they have both helped me to find and love myself.

My mother is a Mahouca woman. The Mahouca are an ethnic group in Ivory Coast especially known for their women, who have big and strong personalities. My mom is no exception. She is a proud African woman who knows how to speak her mother tongue, Mahouca, because when she was little she lived in a house where people spoke it just as much as French.

My mom never taught my sister and me Mahouca, as the circumstances weren't conducive. Her mother tongue was different from my dad's, and when I was young, she was careful about not pushing her culture on my sister and me. Moreover, like many contemporary Ivorians, she grew up somewhat disconnected from her family—and over time, she stopped doing anything that revealed her attachment to them. She'd grown up in the countryside, and the transition to "modern" life in the city I grew up in often brought with it the erasure of traditional habits. Because of colonization, we were around only French-speaking people, and I know my mom felt that learning and speaking Mahouca at home might have been confusing to me and my sister. Still, while many of the people around us considered it low class to speak one's mother tongue, my mom taught me to love hers and to recognize the beauty of African languages.

My mom and I have similar personalities, which means our relationship wasn't always easy in my teenage years and we butted heads quite a bit. I didn't always feel understood by her, but at the same time, she regularly came through for me and offered me support in the most important ways. I always felt assured that I could safely talk with her and share intimate information without being yelled at or judged. Unfortunately, African parents are known for being strict and closed-minded and not particularly open to discussion. I am blessed that my mother is not like this.

My mom has always been interested in beauty. Feeling beautiful makes her feel happy and at home with herself. One thing I admire about her is that she was and still is always on point. Even when she stayed home all day, she'd walk around with lovely clothes, gorgeous hair, and immaculate makeup. When I was younger, I believed that doing all of these things meant you simply wanted attention and appreciation from others; I couldn't see how taking pride in one's appearance for its own sake could be a marker of confidence. (I soon came to realize that my mom was absolutely confident without any of those external things, as she was fine going without makeup if she didn't have the time!)

I loved watching my mother's daily ritual, which would take more than an hour each day. She'd wake up, put on a face peel and a face mask, drink her coffee, take a shower, and finally apply her makeup, do her hair, and dress up. She seemed to know all the best products for skincare and haircare (generally, all natural). She was one of my earliest influences when it came to my love for the fashion industry and the world of beauty. Seeing her pamper herself with so much love and care during my childhood planted a seed of awareness within me. I came to recognize that instead of being hard on ourselves, we must do what we can to cherish our bodies in ways that affirm who we are.

On my bad days, when I was feeling my worst, my mom would always tell me how beautiful I was and would compliment my skin and my features, as well as my intelligence and other positive attributes. I knew she was being completely honest, too. She would hype me up when I tried on new clothes or hairstyles, and her attitude helped me grow my self-confidence and my willingness to be visible and celebrated for who I am.

After her divorce from my dad, my mom worked extremely hard to take care of my sister and me and to make our lives happy and comfortable. Even when she was tired and emotionally drained, she tried her best to share special moments with us. She was my first female role model: an exemplar of strength and determination who fought to give us everything we needed.

My little sister, Florencia, is five years younger than me. She is a little calmer than my mom and me, but she still has a strong personality. It seems to run in the family! Like most siblings, we used to fight a lot, but we shared almost everything and developed an unbreakable bond. Florencia is my best friend. She has always shown me support and been enthusiastic about my achievements and dreams, and I in turn have done the same for her.

When we were children, Florencia always looked up to me: she wanted to dress like me, do the same activities, and so on. I found that annoying, but it was also a source of self-confidence. I felt a strong sense of responsibility as the older sister, and I knew I had to set a good example for her. I had to do my best to show her what a woman's confidence looks like, so that she could grow up to be the best version of herself.

Today, the three of us—my mom, my sister, and I—are extremely close. Moments of disagreement don't last long, and we continue to share almost everything. The feeling of safety I experience with them is incomparable, and I know they will always love me. This bond was my first experience of deep sisterhood, and I am so fortunate to have grown up with an understanding of the power of women supporting and uplifting one another. My relationship with them helped me to see the women around me as allies instead of competition. My mother, my sister, and I have shared so many moments, so many experiences, so many highs and lows, and we continue to grow throughout all of this. They are my blood, as well as my heart and joy. I know without a doubt that their happiness is mine, and mine is theirs.

I started doing my sister Florencia's hair when I was nine years old and she was just four. I loved to braid her hair, and she was the only person willing to give me her head to experiment on! When I wasn't working on her hair, I was doing it on my dolls.

I loved putting extensions in my sister's hair, as well as doing cornrows and twists and coming up with all kinds of other styles. I remember her smile each time I finished her hair and she examined the result in the mirror. She was always so happy, even when my efforts weren't all that great due to my lack of dexterity. (After all, I was only nine!) She was always so encouraging, and this shared ritual of hair braiding helped us to develop an unbreakable bond as sisters. And even today, she still occasionally lets me do her hair!

THE FIGHT FOR JUSTICE AND THE EQUALITY OF SEXES

Reconnecting with my African roots turned me toward feminism. As I learned to appreciate my culture, my hair, my skin, my body, and my beautiful African features—all of which are such important parts of me—I realized that I was worthy of existing. My insecurities didn't disappear with a snap of my fingers, but appreciating all the different facets that make me *me* helped me learn to love one more vital thing: being a woman.

Ivorian society, like so many societies, is very misogynistic. Sexism is so normalized that women learn to live with it. We internalize it. I now recognize this as a way of reconciling one's identity and role within the world...a way of surviving in an environment that might not be very kind to you.

I was born into a patriarchal system, and the difference in the treatment of boys and girls was always obvious to me. I grew up learning that men were the chiefs, while women were expected to follow their rules. I was taught that my most important dream was supposed to be getting married and having a family of my own. Even when I recognized the unfairness of sex roles, I never really stopped to question them. I internalized double standards, and I absorbed the message that violence against women was normal, sometimes even justified.

People who experience oppression and abuse grow accustomed to being belittled and treated as second-class citizens and learn to accept maltreatment, bullying, and martyrdom. Our own self-perception is distorted. We often suffer from impostor syndrome, and the insecurities we harbor can fester and silence us when we internalize the belief that we don't deserve happiness.

I know, because I went through all of this.

I learned that loving yourself is a path to learning how to fight and to stand up for yourself and others who have experienced injustice and oppression. When you know without a doubt that you are worthy, you no longer accept the world as it is; you realize you have a responsibility to change it.

I remained quiet for too long, but as soon as I began to realize my worth as a human being, I began to ask myself: *Who made up all of these rules?* Suddenly, I was starting to notice all the injustices to which I was subject, merely because I was born female and African.

My mom played a huge role in my awakening to feminism and social justice. After she divorced my dad, I recognized in her a strong woman who had to do almost everything she could to support my little sister and me, financially and otherwise. She worked to progressively improve our lives, even though society had told her that her duty was only to cook, clean, and take care of her household. She was so much bigger than our indoctrinated ideas of who a woman should be. My mom opened my eyes to our potential as women and human beings, and our power to seize that potential—for ourselves and for others. I long to tell the stories of all the other women who suffer because their fates have been taken out of their hands and placed in those of a culture that does not value their freedom and choice.

Everyday Sexism

Sexism doesn't always manifest as violent behavior toward women. It can be subtle and scarcely noticeable, which makes it all the more vicious because it's difficult to identify.

Even the most privileged among us face the realities of everyday sexism, which encompasses derogatory language, stereotypes, words, gestures, and acts that exclude, infantilize, marginalize, belittle, destabilize, and delegitimize women. It is present everywhere: home, work, school, advertising, education, and even among women who are the recipients of this mistreatment. Everyday sexism includes:

- The myth of the "maternal instinct"—the idea that women are naturally inclined to care for children. Often, women like myself who don't want children are viewed as unnatural and selfish, although men who express the same sentiment are never questioned.
- The expectation that women will ultimately leave a job in order to have children, leading to women being passed over for positions or promotions in favor of men.
- The demand for women to "smile because it makes you look prettier"—which perpetuates the toxic belief that women are ornaments to be looked at and admired rather than individuals with a right to their own feelings and expression.

"I only know that people call me a feminist whenever I express sentiments that differentiate me from a doormat." —Rebecca West

Many women are ashamed to call themselves feminists because of the negative connotations that patriarchy has given to this word. But being a feminist just means you want women to be treated like human beings, with our dignity intact and our rights acknowledged. Being a feminist means you want to fight injustice and stand up for yourself and other women. Feminism is ultimately about our power to choose who we are and who we wish to be, on our own terms. Feminism is about equality—that's what makes it a powerful concept instead of a dirty word.

- The patronizing and condescending attitudes displayed toward women—for example, when men help women lift objects even when they don't need help or when they interrupt or speak over women.
- The assumption that if a woman has luxury items, a man must have bought them for her—an assumption I've often faced personally!

In many parts of the world, including Ivory Coast, women are expected to be the caretakers of the home: the ones who cook, clean, do the dishes and laundry, and see to the needs of the children and the overall household. But our potential is so much bigger, and we have the right to move beyond expected roles and explore all of who we are.

A few years ago, my boyfriend at the time accompanied me to a big market in Abidjan where people go when they want to haggle for a good price on a new phone or technological accessories. I'd planned to pay for my phone myself, of course, but I wasn't very good at negotiating prices, so I'd brought my boyfriend along to help me. He was able to obtain a lower price than what I'd expected, so I was happy. The seller turned to my boyfriend and said, "You're a good guy! This phone is very expensive, and it's a beautiful gift for your girlfriend." He then turned to me and said, "You'd better keep him! He wouldn't buy you such a gift if he didn't love you." The seller had automatically assumed that my boyfriend was paying for the phone, and I said nothing. Worse, I handed my money to my boyfriend under the table so he wouldn't be embarrassed.

This is what everyday sexism does to us: seemingly harmless words and actions coerce even the most independent of women to act in ways that go against our better instincts...for the sake of conforming to sex stereotypes that do not ultimately serve any of us.

Benevolent sexism is the attitude that women need protection and assistance because they are fragile, demure, or incompetent. This "chivalry" is like a pair of golden handcuffs. The small advantages offered by benevolent sexism are meant to keep us from revolting against injustice and inequality. Benevolent sexism is a vicious and illusory system intended to make a woman feel lucky to be treated well, only to silence her if she is abused.

The Cost of Internalized Misogyny

There are a lot of ugly stereotypes about women—that we are catty or untrustworthy, and that we fight over men. We are painted as merciless bullies and "mean girls"—the way people talk about us, you'd think we were biologically wired that way.

For years, I held misconceptions about who I am and what I deserve as a woman. The idea that men are superior to women was ingrained so deeply that it simply became a part of my inner landscape. As a teenager, I found myself casting sexist judgments on other girls for the way they looked, the way they talked and behaved, and the way they existed—especially if they were breaking the rules of womanhood as I'd learned them.

I saw other girls and women as my competition, and because they treated me the same way, we all became both perpetrators and victims of sexism. For if you constantly judge yourself as the inferior sex, you will inevitably project your insecurities and negative judgments onto other women. We start to buy into the stereotypes and ask: *Who is the prettiest? Who is the most desirable? Who will be married quickly?* We objectify one another. We learn that we need to wear makeup and be pretty (but not too pretty, otherwise we will be seen as vain), dress well (but not too provocatively, for danger of being labeled a "slut"), be sexy (but not too sexy, or our "virtue" will be called into question), be smart (but not too smart, because that isn't considered feminine), and express confidence (but not too much confidence, because we don't want to come across as overbearing or like we don't need men).

Because we are indoctrinated to believe in our inferiority, it's no wonder women grow up fighting over the attention and love of men! After all, we are taught that men will protect us—financially, physically, and otherwise. Our priority is to attract and keep a man, even when they display violence toward us.

This leads us to be toxic competitors in other aspects of life. In high school, I was jealous if I came in second in my class and another girl came in first, but it didn't trouble me if a boy happened to be in the same position. I was fine with men being better than me, but I had to be the best woman. Life was a zero-sum game, and there was surely not enough space for all women to achieve excellence.
Of course, none of this is to blame women for falling prey to sexism and misogyny. It is not easy to deconstruct these beliefs. They

are part of our reality, like the air we breathe and the water we drink, and men, too, have a duty to dismantle oppression of all kinds—especially when they inhabit a place of power and privilege.

These days, I don't see women as competition. I see them as my sisters and allies. I believe the only way to dismantle sexism is for women to come together. Society depends on oppressed groups remaining separated and powerless; on our own, we are vulnerable and incapable of sufficiently fighting injustice. But together? We can move mountains. If feelings of jealousy arise, I acknowledge them but I don't give in to them—because I know that the world I want to be a part of creating is one in which we all have equal opportunities. Instead of continuing the cycle of misogyny, together we can eradicate the conditions that make it possible.

Who Gets to Define Womanhood?

Femininity is a set of characteristics, behaviors, and physical and mental qualities that society has commonly associated with women and girls. It's a socially defined set of norms that covers everything from behavior and personality to taste in clothing and fashion to appearance. Depending on a woman's proximity to femininity, she might be judged or her womanhood could be called into question. Ironically, she may face judgment if she is "unfeminine," but at the same time, qualities associated with femininity (including gentleness, passivity, and beauty—but also cattiness, untrustworthiness, and fickleness) are often minimized or demonized. It's yet another case of "damned if you do, damned if you don't."

Ideals of femininity fluctuate depending on time and culture, but "masculine" and "feminine" qualities live inside every one of us. How we choose to express ourselves—in our style of speaking, dressing, or anything else—should never be used against us to prove or deny our womanhood. Womanhood is unique to every single woman. A woman has the right to relate—or not relate—to the concept of femininity, but let's keep in mind that whatever she decides, she will never be less of a woman, because "femininity" has nothing to be with being a woman. Womanhood doesn't require following any rules or stereotypes. Whether we prefer to don dresses or pants, wear our hair short or long, gravitate toward activities perceived as "unsuitable" for our sex or not—we have the right to let our true selves shine through and to embrace our womanhood on our own terms!

The Ever-Present Double Standard

Double standards about the conduct of men and women are extremely prevalent in Ivory Coast. Since childhood, I've witnessed how boys and girls are treated differently for the same actions, and how different rules are applied. I experienced this myself, and it took me a long time to recognize that this was far from OK.

Even our language demonstrates double standards. Men and boys might be labeled "passionate" and "enthusiastic"; girls and women with the same qualities might be viewed as "over-emotional" or even "crazy." It is seen as perfectly acceptable for men to express their anger, even in dramatic ways; women who do the same are in danger of being labeled "hysterical" or even "dangerous." The quality of "leadership" in a man or boy translates to "bossiness" in a woman or girl, and extroversion, assertiveness, decisiveness, and high self-regard are often demonized in women.

As someone with a naturally strong personality, I find it very difficult to live under the expectation that I must always be soft, quiet, polite, and docile. Likewise, I imagine that boys with a gentle disposition are shamed for being "effeminate" or "less of a man." These labels perpetuate patriarchy and keep all of us, men and women, from expressing the full spectrum of who we are.

The Valorization of Boy Babies over Girl Babies

In Ivory Coast and in many other places around the world, the life of a little girl does not have the same value as that of a little boy. Often, discovering that a woman will be giving birth to a boy is considered a benediction. The same pride is absent when there is news of a girl.

Many men will blame women if they birth only girls, even though it is a man's sperm that determines the sex of his child. Some men will divorce their wives for not birthing boys, or they will use this as an excuse to take a second wife.

Young girls have the same worth as young boys, and they are just as much of a blessing to their families. They deserve to be loved, valued, heard, and cared for. Women absolutely should have the right to make the personal choice to have an abortion, but with sex-selective abortion, that choice is rooted in devaluing the female sex. Abortion should not arise from societal discrimination.

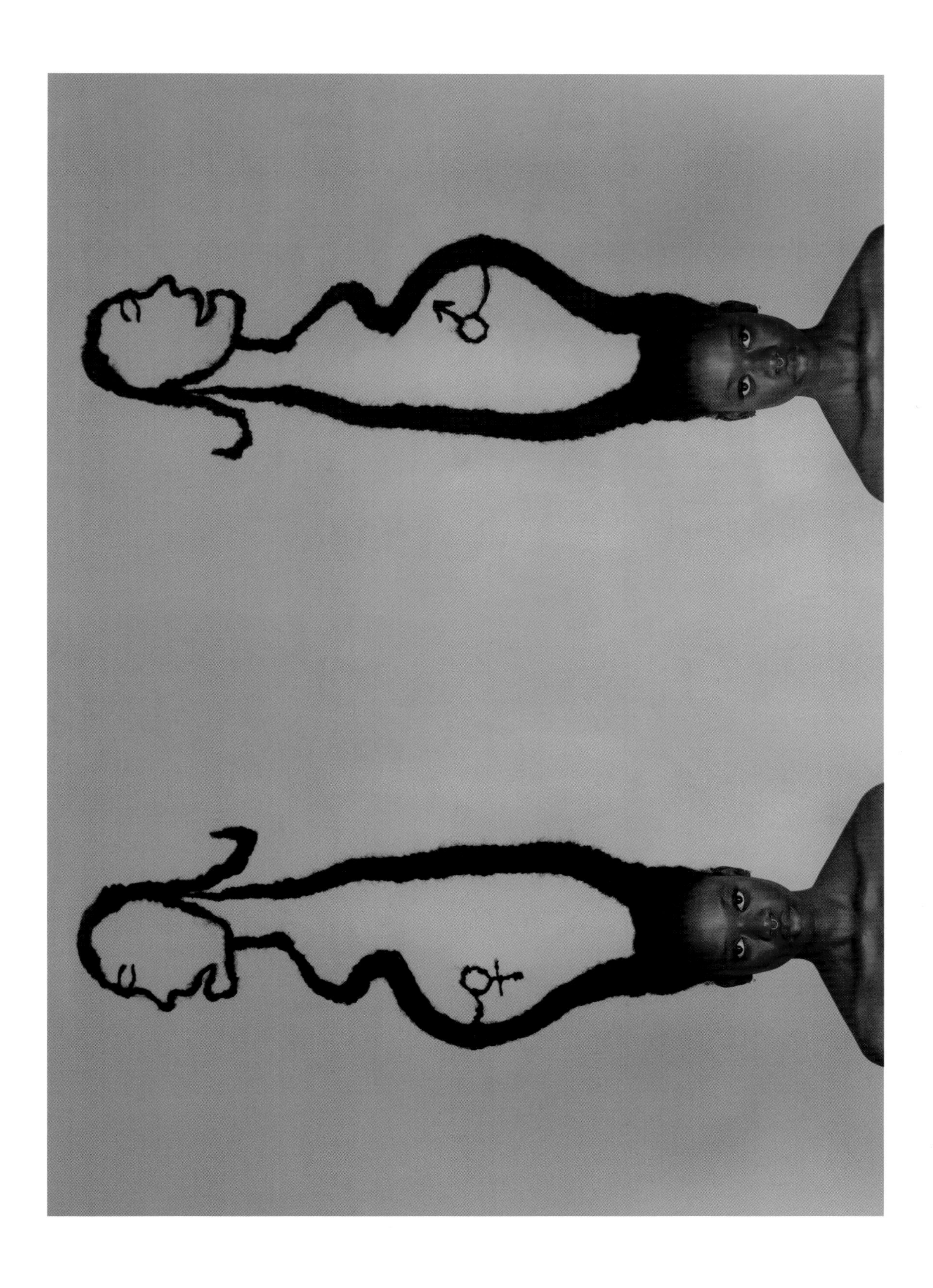

Boys vs. Girls

Growing up with only a sister, I didn't witness double standards in my own home: Florencia and I were treated the same way and received the same amount of love. I first realized that boys and girls weren't treated the same when my parents separated and my sister and I moved temporarily into my maternal grandmother's house, which was located conveniently close to our school. Florencia and I became part of a household with three other elementary school-aged cousins: a girl and two boys. I was shocked to discover that the boys were pampered and didn't have to do any chores at home. We had to learn how to cook and clean, while the boys were excused from this drudgery. After everyone ate, the girls were expected to do the dishes while the boys sat around doing nothing. And if the boys were loud or violent, their behavior was tolerated, but when the girls behaved the same way, there were always consequences.

Moreover, the girls' punishment was much more severe if we neglected these chores the same way the boys did. Once, because I forgot to clean the bathroom as my grandma had requested, I was spanked. The boys' bedroom and bathroom were always dirty, yet nobody said anything to them. Instead, a housekeeper did all of their cleaning for them. Even at school, all the girls were charged with taking a broom to clean the classroom each morning while the boys remained outside, waiting for us to finish.

Girls also seem to receive less love and kindness. They are expected to take on a more adult role early in life, while boys are afforded the luxury of "just being boys." While boys' toys range from cars to robots to fighting figurines, girls are given dolls, mini-kitchens, and beauty accessories to prepare them for their future roles. Their hopes, dreams, and ambitions are not nurtured or stimulated. And for most girls, it becomes easier to resign themselves to their fate than to fight it.

If we want a better world for women, we need to eliminate the difference in how we educate our boys and our girls. Outdated and arbitrary double standards only condition young people to perpetuate patriarchy.

The Power (and Absence) of Education

In Ivory Coast, there is a huge disparity in literacy rates between the sexes. Roughly 63.7 percent of women and 46.75 percent of men are illiterate, according to Ivory Coast's National Institute of Statistics. This disparity is fairly consistent in many parts of the world.

When I look at these numbers, I come to the conclusion that as a nation and as a world, we don't want women to think, to reflect, and to have aspirations. In many places, women are expected to forego their education altogether so they can stay home, cook, clean, and make children. In rural areas, it's even worse. Girls labor in the fields while boys receive an education.

When I was ten years old, I was very close to the woman who was paid to take care of me while my parents were at work. She was quite young, perhaps twenty-five, and one day when she asked me to read out loud a message she'd received on her mobile phone, I realized that she couldn't read. I was surprised, so I asked her why. She told me her parents decided to keep her out of school because they thought it would be a waste of time and money, since she would end up married to a man who would take care of her financially. She would be better off at home, learning to cook, clean, and manage a household. Her parents invested in schooling her two brothers because, unlike her, they would need to earn money to take care of their future wives and families.

A man in her village who was much older wanted to marry her when she was eighteen. Her parents accepted without her consent because he was wealthy. She stayed with him for two years, and then she became sick. For a long period, she was unable to cook or take care of him, so he kicked her out of his home and took another wife.

She was forced to go back to her parents' home to recover. She had a child, so it would be hard to find another man who would want her. Her parents became bothered by her "useless" presence in their home, so she decided to go to the city to build a better life for herself and her child. Due to her lack of education, she was forced to do menial jobs until she found the position in my family's home through a nanny agency. She told me her goal was to stay for a year and save enough money to start a small business.

I was confused. I'd grown up in a modern household that didn't harbor the same toxic stereotypes about sex roles. I couldn't imagine that in the same country where I lived, other women were being subjected to such horrible and disempowering conditions.

After she left, most of the women who came to work in our home as cooks or nannies couldn't read, either. Generally, they had chosen their occupation because it was one of a very small handful of career opportunities for women lacking a proper education. Their stories were all similar: most had families who didn't think it was necessary to put a girl through school.

Clearly, given that so many of these women had married men who didn't provide for them as they'd been taught to expect, the collective decision to limit young girls' education is misguided and harmful. Women are being raised to form an unhealthy dependency on men who may not value their well-being: without a proper education, these women's options are severely limited. I taught some of the women who came into our home how to read, but it was heartbreaking to see how difficult their lives were because their families clung to the outdated and incorrect belief that women don't need to be educated.

Double Standards in the Workplace

In Ivory Coast, as in most parts of the world, men are much better paid than women for the same work. Once, I applied for a business internship in a company I chose specifically because one of my friends, a man, had informed me that interns were well paid. My friend and I had the same level of experience: we were in our second year of college, and we both had high grades. They offered to give me only a small stipend for transportation, whereas my male friend was given a salary. I needed the internship to validate my second year of college, so I accepted it, despite my disappointment and sense of injustice.

Similarly, my mother was working in a company where she had performed excellently—which many of her colleagues and other managers recognized. She put in a lot of effort to get a promotion. She wanted to become a manager, but that role was given to a man

A society cannot truly call itself "developed" if half of the population is marginalized or has limited access to opportunities. It makes no sense *not* to give women the full opportunity to express our potential in the professional world.

with fewer achievements who was less competent and experienced. My mom cried profusely, not understanding why she was passed over. A few months later, she heard the president of the company say he could never hire a woman as a manager because she wouldn't have the same authority as a man and would not be respected by her subordinates.

The wage gap affects not only urban women like myself or my mom but also women in villages and small towns. Women compose the largest labor force in Ivory Coast. Almost everywhere, women work and men reap the benefits of their work by pocketing all of their wives' wages. Despite women's industriousness, it seems as though we always bump up against a cold, hard glass ceiling.

Women and Sexuality

Double standards around sex naturally infiltrate intimacy, sexuality, and relationships. The ways in which men and women are judged for their actions in the context of a sexual relationship are so numerous that I can't begin to name them here. But the effects are deep and toxic, and for fear of being labeled a "slut," women tend to approach their relationships with a great deal of caution.

What people expect from a good wife is very different from what people expect from a good husband. In Ivory Coast, it's considered par for the course for a man to cheat. The stereotype that men are inherently sexual and have the innate biological need to spread their seed enables people to excuse men's cheating. They don't even bother to hide it, as there are no repercussions for such behavior. Sometimes, they even talk about it with pride. They refer to their main woman as *premier bureau* ("first office") and their side chick as *deuxième bureau* ("second office"), but a woman who dares to juggle multiple relationships is often mistreated, humiliated, beaten, and socially ostracized.

Women, too, have sexual desires that we are capable of separating from love—and we may not want to be tied down in an intimate relationship if we have other priorities. We should not have to hide our sex and love lives to live up to society's double standards.

When I was younger, one of my aunts decided to divorce her abusive husband because he got another woman pregnant. Everyone made her feel like she was being selfish for leaving—they didn't think it was a valid reason for breaking up the marriage.

Another aunt of mine would cry on the phone to express how sad she was about her husband's infidelity. One day, this aunt came to visit us and informed my mom that she'd discovered who the other woman was. Along with a couple of friends, she'd shown up at the woman's home to beat her and keep her away from my aunt's husband once and for all. My mom was shocked and told her this was a poor solution, but my aunt disagreed.

I was confused: I couldn't understand why my aunt was so angry at this woman but seemed not to be upset with her husband at all. In fact, her love for him seemed stronger than ever! My aunt declared that it was the woman's fault because she could have said no when she was approached by a married man. So although her husband had clearly orchestrated this entire situation, my aunt blamed the other woman for not exercising self-control!

Many husbands lie to their mistresses about their situation, pretending they are single or about to get a divorce, so often neither woman knows the full truth—both women have been wronged. But when the cards get laid out on the table, very few people sympathize with the side chick. Our society's internalized misogyny has led us to absorb the toxic double standard without even recognizing it.

The sexual double standard is an extreme example of society's contradictory expectations for men and women. A woman with a "high body count"—that is, who's had sex with many people—is considered a "whore," while a man with a high body count is viewed as a champion; a woman's virginity adds "value" to her existence. Women's masturbation is considered diabolical, taboo, strange, and perverse, while self-pleasuring is normalized for a man. And a woman having sex on the first date is "easy" and lacks virtue, but a man in the same shoes is a lucky guy. I remember having an argument with a man I was interested in because I was honest with him about my body count. Even though his was higher, he immediately became cold and hostile. He told me he wasn't sure he wanted to date me because, according to him, I didn't respect my body enough. I responded that I was absolutely sure I didn't want to date him because of his disgusting reaction.

Another time, I was shamed for my sexual behavior when I went to a pharmacy to pay for a morning-after pill. I was about seventeen years old. The male pharmacist made a very sexist comment to the effect of: "If you weren't sleeping with men, you wouldn't need this. This is why we tell young girls to focus on their studies." Some of the employees and shoppers overheard him, which was mortifying. To this day, I regret remaining silent as this stranger berated me.

When a young woman buys condoms, the reactions are often similar. She receives a lot of judgment, with the reasoning that she isn't pure enough or doesn't respect herself enough, but I suspect that much of that judgment has to do with women assuming agency and power. A woman who makes her own decisions is seen as disrupting the status quo. A woman who sits in the recognition that her body and her desires belong to her alone is viewed as dangerous.

Sexualization of the Female Body

Although women's sexuality is taboo, this doesn't prevent our bodies and behaviors from being sexualized. The early sexualization of young girls' bodies has major effects on our physical and mental health. All over the world, this objectification, which we internalize in our later years, results in lack of self-confidence, discomfort with our bodies, anxiety and depression, an unhealthy relationship with our sexuality, eating disorders, and all kinds of misconceptions and distorted beliefs about womanhood. Sexualization also makes women vulnerable to abuse, harassment, and sexual violence.

By no means am I suggesting that women don't have the right to display themselves as sexy or even to make money off their own image. I am simply saying that it is not a society's role to do that for women. All of us should have the freedom to decide how we want to dress and what image we want to convey, whether on social media or elsewhere. This should not be determined by arbitrary standards of beauty and sexuality.

BE SEXY
AND SHUT UP

Censorship and Body Shaming

As an artist, I believe the female body is one of the most beautiful forms that exists. The female body represents the processes of creation, which are not limited to motherhood. I am against censorship of the female body, in all its diverse expressions.

This censorship is ironic, considering that society is also responsible for sexualizing the female body. In some parts of the world, women can't even breastfeed their babies—one of the most natural and primal of human activities—in public. Women's bodies are also censored on social media, television, and film; this censorship conveniently ends when individuals and corporations can monetize female sexuality. It is a vicious circle: the more our bodies are censored, the more sexualized and taboo they become—and the more our bodies are sexualized and seen as taboo, the more they are censored.

For centuries in much of traditional African society, the female body was considered natural and neutral. It was not sexualized or demonized. However, colonization and Western attitudes toward "primitive" African behavior—as well as the associated fear of Black bodies and Black sexuality—have conditioned us as Africans to believe that tribes where women live bare-chested are "savage" and "uncivilized." We proclaim all of this while glorifying our own society, in which men can't be expected to control themselves in front of a woman whose breasts are exposed.

When I stopped wearing a bra because it was so uncomfortable, I was not prepared for all the unsolicited comments from men about my nipples. I have small breasts with average nipples that tend to be prominent through my shirt. There is an Ivorian song called "Bobitana," which translates to "little pointy breasts." It's a very sexist song that objectifies girls with small breasts. One day while I was out walking, a group of young men started following me, singing this song out loud together. It was extremely embarrassing. I was lucky because my car wasn't far away, so I was able to make a quick escape.

Another time, I was kicked out of a college class because my nipples were noticeable. The inspector who was walking around to ensure we were all doing

Women's nudity is often equated with pornography—especially on social media, where images of the female body are monitored and censored more closely than even hate speech. But our bodies are not objects—they are expressions of our autonomy and vehicles for our powerful spirits!

Young girls who are just developing a sense of self often endure bullying that is centered on body shaming. The effects can be disastrous, potentially spurring acts of self-harm and even suicide. I know from firsthand experience that body shame can impact a woman's entire life: if you don't feel good in your body, you will not feel good in your mind.

our work told me I needed to go and change my shirt. She said, "You are dressed too provocatively, and this might distract your teacher." I was wearing a simple shirt with long sleeves. But there was nothing I could do to respond to this ludicrous remark. I had no choice but to obey.

Reproductive Rights

Reproductive rights are essential human rights, protected by regional and international treaties, as well as national laws. They embrace the right of all individuals and couples to decide whether to have children, as well as the number and timing of their children. They include offering people sex education and the information to help them make the best decisions about their bodies, sexuality, and sexual health, free of violence and coercion. Reproductive rights extend to the ability to use contraceptives, to terminate a pregnancy, and to access reproductive health services. (In Ivory Coast, women face limited access to reproductive health services and don't have the right to make informed decisions about their bodies, as abortion is not legal.)

Sex Education

An effective sex education enables young people and even adults to adopt positive sexual behavior. By increasing knowledge about reproduction and sexuality, good sex education can improve people's attitudes toward their bodies while decreasing the possibility of risky behavior.

Unfortunately, there is a big taboo concerning sex education in Ivory Coast. Adults think that talking about sex with children encourages them to have sex. Their idea of meaningful sex education is to warn their child to remain abstinent until marriage. Most young people pick up "knowledge" about sex from television, pornography, and their peers—which can have disastrous consequences.

Even in schools, sex education is distorted and incomplete, so that when young people decide to have sex, they are not properly informed. They have no idea about the kinds of infections they could contract or the precautions to prevent them. Women tend to be the most impacted, as many get pregnant while they are still in school, which forces them to stop their education altogether.

I have a friend who was so ignorant about everything concerning sex that the first time she had her period at the age of twelve, she cried because another ignorant child had told her that periods only came after a woman had sex. Naturally, my friend was confused and thought she would be in trouble because her mom would think she'd had sex.

Young people who are not educated about sex grow into ignorant adults—and I have met a lot of them. I had a partner who thought if a woman is lubricated, neither person can contract HIV/AIDS or other STIs. He was twenty-five. I was shocked when he told me he had never used condoms because all his partners had always been sufficiently wet. When I explained to him how things really worked, he was genuinely surprised.

Birth Control

Africa, with the world's highest rates of fertility as well as maternal and infant mortality, is also home to the lowest rates of contraceptive use. Only around 15 percent of all women in West Africa use modern birth control techniques; many women who resort to an abortion don't have access to contraceptives or have experienced failure when using the rhythm method.

In Ivory Coast, birth control is available in the largest city, but in the villages, it is virtually nonexistent. In addition, the types of contraception are limited, the available services are poor quality, and women—especially young ones—who inquire about contraception are persistently shamed and stigmatized for even considering sexual intercourse. Even when a mature woman wishes to use contraception, some people will insist this is sinful, because they believe God desires us to procreate.

Women in villages give birth to an average of twelve children before the age of thirty. My own great-grandmother had fifteen children. In rural areas, married women often become pregnant again shortly after giving birth due to a lack of contraception. This can result in serious health consequences for the woman and her children.

Most women don't choose to have children; they have them because there is no alternative. Some don't even know that having children can be avoided through birth control. For us to live in truly equitable and anti-oppressive societies, we must ensure that women have agency over their own bodies, as well as meaningful education and access to birth control.

Abortion

In Ivory Coast, religious lobbyists have blocked pro-choice legislation. Because abortion is illegal, the few doctors who safely offer it are extremely expensive. Young girls who lack the money to safely terminate a pregnancy resort to dangerous alternatives, including the introduction of metallic objects and unsterilized instruments into the uterus by people who are not medical professionals, as well as the ingestion of plants and synthetic substances without the proper guidance of a medical professional. The results of these procedures can range from hemorrhages to genital lesions to infection from a perforated uterus to other often-unacknowledged forms of medical trauma. Some women lose the ability to procreate altogether or even die.

When I was in my last year of high school, a close friend of mine got pregnant. My friend didn't want the baby. She knew that neither she nor her boyfriend was ready for the responsibility and that they couldn't afford it. She was a brilliant student, and she planned to continue her studies abroad after graduating high school. A child would have destroyed all her plans.

My friend knew she couldn't confide in her parents, who were extremely religious. Not only would they have been deeply disappointed in her, they also would have forced her to keep the baby. She wanted to end the pregnancy without telling her parents, but she didn't have the money for a proper abortion. Neither did her boyfriend. Still, she was determined. It took my friend three attempts to terminate the pregnancy—not to mention, a roller coaster of emotions and a painful infection.

My friend first tried a mixture of three different medicines suggested by a friend who said she'd used them to end her own pregnancy. However, after days of heavy bleeding and losing her vitality, my friend discovered she was still pregnant. Desperate to find another solution, she then tried a plant potion sold by a man in a market—we didn't even know what was in this dark-green, horrendous-smelling mixture. She was supposed to drink it every day at the same hour for three days. Every time, my friend experienced a horrible pain so strong that she would vomit right afterward. But nothing changed: she remained pregnant.

While many people seem to care about the viability of a fetus, this care clearly does not extend to the many abandoned or abused children in our world. To be truly pro-life is to genuinely care for the life that is already in this world. Women are not beasts of burden who should be coerced into birthing children. Our uteruses, our choice.

She decided to do something even more drastic for her last attempt: she went to a woman who was known for performing low-cost abortions. This woman wasn't a doctor or even in the medical field. I accompanied my friend to the woman's home; after a few minutes, I heard a loud scream; the woman hadn't used an anesthetic. I didn't know what her method was, since I was not allowed into the room.

The woman came out and gestured to me to come and take my friend. When I entered the room, I was horrified. My friend was lying there, unconscious. I screamed in alarm, and the woman immediately told me to shut up. She didn't seem to be worried in the least—she just reassured me that my friend would get up soon and then asked who was going to pay. Fortunately, a few minutes later, my friend got up. She couldn't walk properly, but the woman insisted that we leave quickly because another client was waiting.

I felt traumatized by this experience—and of course, my trauma didn't even compare to my friend's. But her parents never found out about the abortion, and she was able to study abroad. She was very lucky to escape major consequences—but this is not the case for many women in the same predicament. The illegality of abortions will never decrease the number of women who need them; it simply puts these women's lives in danger. It is important to protect these women by making abortion legal and offering safe, medically sound procedures to those who wish to exercise agency over their bodies.

Violence Against Women

Violence against women can take many different forms: it can be physical harm (beating, strangling, pushing, using a weapon), sexual harm (primarily, attempting to obtain sex coercively, without consent), and psychological harm (ranging from verbal abuse and insults to economic violence and control).

Not only does patriarchy silence women when they are abused, but it also gaslights them into believing that they deserve the abuse. Every single woman deserves a life free of violence—and she has the right to assert this, loudly and clearly. It can be scary to call out an aggressor, and many times, women don't even have the opportunity. However, if we want things to change, we must speak out and tell our stories.

Speech is a powerful weapon and the first step toward change. Let's inspire women all over the world to shrug off the burden of silence when they are undergoing abuse and injustice. Let's support our sisters in claiming their right to dignity and freedom from suffering.

Sexism in the Family

Men are disproportionately praised for taking care of their children, while women are generally expected to be natural caregivers and are not often accorded the same appreciation. A woman taking care of her babies is simply doing what is expected of her, but a man who does the same is lauded as an exceptional, engaged dad who deserves a medal for his attentiveness.

I remember talking to an ex-boyfriend who said he wanted to have babies with me. He knew I wasn't at all excited about that prospect, so he tried to convince me that I didn't have to worry because he'd help take care of our "future children." I was genuinely surprised that he considered taking care of his own children to be helping his partner. But society praises men so much for doing the bare minimum that basic fatherly behavior is perceived as kind or even heroic. Women are conditioned to believe it's their sole responsibility to take care of the children, so if their male partners participate in a few parenting tasks, they actually consider themselves lucky!

Men with children are expected to have a social life outside the home with their friends, while women on a girls' night out are seen as selfish, negligent mothers. This double standard makes women feel guilty when they decide to put themselves first. Once, when I was dressed up and ready to dance and have fun with a group of girlfriends, I could see that one of my friends—the mother of a one-year-old—was clearly not having a good time. Although she'd been enthusiastic in the group chat leading up to that night, she admitted to me, "I feel like I shouldn't be here while my son is at home with my mom. He needs me! And to be honest, this is the first time I've gone out since he was born." She couldn't fathom going out and having a life beyond her son, even though he was safe at home with another adult. My friend's partner, her child's father, routinely hung out with his friends—and I'm willing to bet he wasn't wasting his time worrying or feeling guilty about his parenting.

A woman has the right to have a life outside of her children. She is first and foremost a human being who needs to sometimes focus her attention and energy on her own life and passions. And children deserve the care of both their parents!

Harassment

Sexual harassment includes acts of verbal and physical aggression, as well as nonverbal acts of a sexual nature that violate the dignity of their recipients. For many of us, harassment begins in our childhood, progresses through our young adulthood, and persists into older age. It can be experienced in any environment: at home, at school, at work, in the streets and on public transportation, and online. Harassers can range from family members to schoolmates to people in positions of power (such as a boss or supervisor) to strangers issuing catcalls on the street.

I can't count the number of times I've been harassed since my very early adolescence. At just twelve years old, I frequently received sexual remarks from grown men. Sometime the harassment was subtle, and other times it was obvious and violating, and it left me in tears and traumatized for days on end.

In my first year of college, one of my teachers made it clear that he was sexually interested in me. I was only sixteen; he was in his fifties. He used to call me into his office and try to engage me in disturbing, inappropriate discussions. He commented on how beautiful I was. He would ask me if I had a boyfriend, if I was interested in older men, and if I'd had sex. He tried to invite me to dinner. Sometimes, he'd even ask me to give him a kiss on the cheek. It was obvious that all of this made me uncomfortable, but it never kept him from taking liberties with me.

I didn't feel like I had much recourse to complain: my word was nothing against his, and speaking up would have destroyed my academic career. Thankfully, I was in his class for only three months, and after I received my final grade, I could simply ignore him.

In numerous other seemingly safe spaces, I've experienced unwanted male attention and sexual harassment. Once, when I was eighteen, I had a horrible toothache that needed urgent attention. My regular dentist wasn't available, so I booked a consultation with another dentist. This new dentist didn't have an assistant, and even before the examination, he was giving me strange looks and smirks. Then, while my mouth was open and immobilized by the dental instruments, he started telling me how beautiful my legs and thighs were. I immediately knew that things would escalate, but he was using sharp tools on my tooth, and I was afraid that he would purposely injure me if I rejected him. So I sat there as patiently as I could, petrified and still, as I waited for him to finish examining my tooth.

Of course, the dentist didn't stop there. "Your boyfriend is lucky to have you," he said as he stroked my hand. I quickly moved my hand, and he told me to not be afraid—he didn't want to hurt me. As soon as he put his tools down, I jumped out of the chair. He quickly grabbed my hand and tried to kiss me. I pushed him away and ran out of the room. I even forgot my insurance card at the reception area because I was so afraid and eager to get away. At that time in my life, I didn't have the confidence or strength to call him out, so I just left and went home, and did my best to forget about him.

Although I am a firm advocate of women having the freedom to express themselves in whatever way they wish, I have learned to carry myself with care. Many years ago, when I went to a popular market in Abidjan wearing a miniskirt, a stranger yelled, "Whore, go put on some clothes!" He approached me very aggressively, saying, "You want to be naked? I will undress you myself." He attempted to actually pull my skirt off, but fortunately, some aunties in the market protected me and chased him away. It was a horrible experience. From that day on, I've always worn pants on excursions to the market.

I have been followed countless times by men who insisted that I give them my phone number. I know how lucky I am that none of these situations ended tragically for me, because this is not the case for many women. In 2019, the case of a man killing a woman after she refused to give him her number made headlines in newspapers across Ivory Coast.

Harassment doesn't happen only in physical spaces; it is ubiquitous online. I continually receive unsolicited photographs of men's genitals. And when I post photos of myself, I receive everything from violent comments from men who are upset by my opinions or the way I flout sexist norms to messages from men who remark that my bodily features make them horny.

Being a woman means living through these aggressions daily. Being ever-vigilant takes a toll on our well-being—it makes us suspicious of people's motives, even in situations where we don't need to be. It perpetuates trauma that is far too easily dismissed as the simple inconveniences of being born a girl.

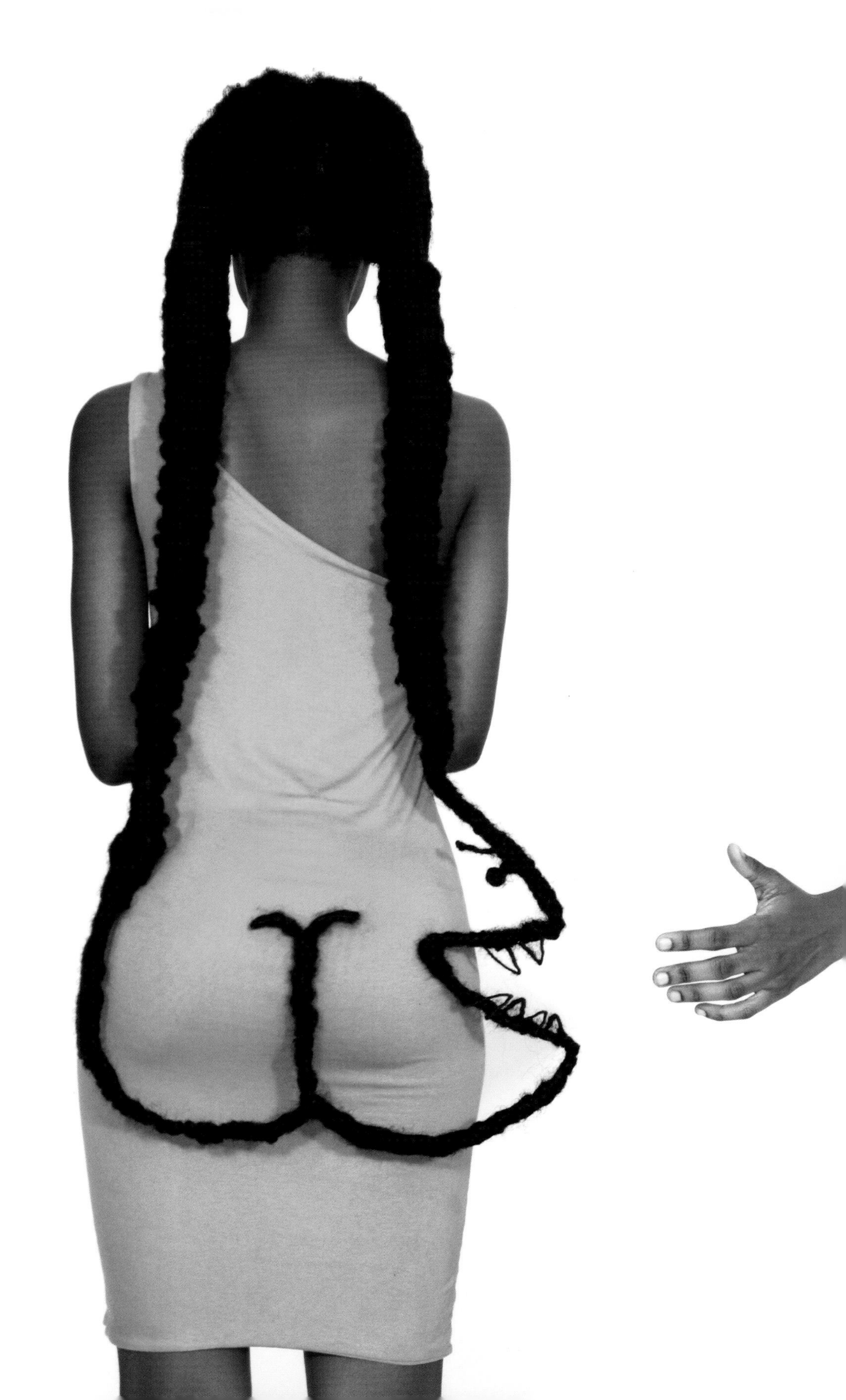

Rape Culture

"Rape culture" is a sociological concept describing an environment in which sexual assault is normalized or trivialized and victims of assault are blamed, especially if they are women. Across the world, many of us are opening our eyes to the fact that rape culture is everywhere—from music and movies and other forms of popular media to the messages we receive from religious and educational institutions.

Rape culture impacts every woman—even those of us who might never have experienced what we consider to be rape. Most women will be subject to misogynistic and abusive language, and to having our bodies objectified. Most women will live in fear of rape, with our sense of mobility and freedom severely limited. The cycle of fear holds us captive, and in many cases, keeps us from speaking out.

One night while I was in college, I was out with some friends celebrating good news, and I drank too much. I don't remember a lot about the evening, but the next day, I woke up on my friend's couch. She explained to me that some boys in our group had been touching me in a sexual way, and she fought them off in order to take me home herself. If she hadn't been there, I would have been alone with the boys after the party. Worst of all, if someone had raped me, the blame would have been placed on my shoulders—because I was drunk. The incident shook me to my core. I decided that day to stop drinking and haven't touched alcohol since. I have to protect myself, even if that means putting my freedoms aside.

Rape culture perpetuates a disregard for women's dignity and right to safety. If someone rapes a woman, people will use the way she dressed, the way she talked to her aggressor, and her proximity to that person to discredit her.

Rape culture is so deeply anchored in Ivory Coast that even some parents don't take the side of their daughter if someone rapes her. Some girls will not speak about being raped because they are afraid they will suffer reprisals: sadly, some parents will kick their daughter out of the house because they believe she sullied the family's name by being raped.

My body belongs to me and only to me. Every single act performed by someone else on me requires my consent.

With many young girls, the rapist is a member of the victim's own family, such as a father, uncle, cousin, or brother. When these cases of incest occur, parents often try to cover up the case to preserve the family's reputation—particularly in cases where the rapist is a family's main provider. The victim's well-being is seldom considered; if anything, these families do whatever they can to avoid the legal system. Most of the time, the aggressor will receive only minor reprimands from the family and will be able to live his life without incident, while the victim will remain traumatized not only by her experience but also by her awareness that the person who harmed her has not been affected at all. These women may not even know that they have a right to justice.

Rape culture is so normalized that many people don't label clearly coercive situations "rape." For example, marital rape is unlawful in Ivory Coast, but most people do not acknowledge it as rape. The same is true of having sex with a drunk or unconscious woman, or someone who has given consent but is under the influence of a drug or mind-altering substance. We don't have language for sex that is obtained through mental manipulation or sex with a minor who has given her consent. And only now are we becoming more aware of the practice known as stealthing—a man removing or damaging a condom during sexual intercourse, to the ignorance of his partner.

We still have a long way to go, but women are gradually learning about the many ways in which rape culture affects and disempowers us on a daily basis—and more of us are coming together in solidarity to talk about our experiences and to fight back.

CONSENT MUST BE VOLUNTARY!

- **If she says no and you insist again and again until she gives in, IT'S RAPE.**
- **If you agree to help her and then demand sex in return, IT'S RAPE.**
- **If you blackmail her emotionally to make her feel guilty for saying no and she ends up saying yes, IT'S RAPE.**
- **If, when she says no, you remind her of anything you've done that might make her feel indebted to you and she then changes her mind, IT'S RAPE.**
- **If you use your strength or position of power to pressure her or scare her into saying yes, IT'S RAPE.**
- **If you hide information that would otherwise change her willingness to consent, IT'S RAPE.**

CONSENT MUST BE CLEAR!

- **Not explicitly saying NO does not necessarily mean yes.**
- **Sexy clothes, accepting an invitation, or wearing makeup is NOT consent.**
- **The fact that she is your girlfriend or your wife does not automatically signal consent.**
- **Anything outside of clear verbal consent is not a yes. Always ask!**

CONSENT MUST BE GIVEN BY SOMEONE WHO CAN CLEARLY OFFER IT!

- **If she's too drunk to consent and she says yes, that doesn't count—IT'S RAPE.**
- **If she is under the effect of a drug or mind-altering substance administered without her knowledge and she says yes, it does not count—IT'S RAPE.**
- **If she is under the age of consent and you're over it, her "yes" does not count—IT'S RAPE.**
- **If she is sleeping or unconscious—IT'S RAPE.**

CONSENT MUST BE SPECIFIC AND GIVEN AT EACH STAGE—AND IT CAN ALSO BE REVOKED AT ANY TIME!

- **If she agrees to make love with you with protection and you remove the condom without her noticing during sexual intercourse, IT'S RAPE.**
- **If you attempt a sexual act without warning and she asks you to stop but you continue, IT'S RAPE.**
- **If, in the middle of a sexual act, she retracts her consent and does not wish to continue but you do so anyway, IT'S RAPE.**

Female Genital Mutilation

Female genital mutilation (FGM) is the practice of partially or totally removing the external genitalia of girls and young women for nonmedical reasons. This sex-based violence typically occurs before a girl reaches puberty. It is a highly dangerous and painful procedure with no religious foundation; however, some communities argue that the ritual derives from their customs and from the belief that it benefits women by keeping them "pure" and virginal.

Although activists in Ivory Coast have fought to ban this practice, young girls continue to be mutilated in many areas of my country. The cutting, which often occurs without anesthesia and by force, is traumatizing—and so are the consequences, which are lifelong. These include severe pain and bleeding, swelling and injury of surrounding genital tissue, scar tissue that does not heal, fever, urinary tract infections, menstrual complications, pain during intercourse, the inability to experience sexual pleasure, increased risk of childbirth complications, and even death. This doesn't begin to address the psychological impacts of living with FGM.

Even though women themselves often preside over the ritual, this custom reflects a society's sexism and misogyny. One of the primary motivations behind FGM is the desire to control women's sexuality. Many people believe that a woman who enjoys sex is dangerous, as she will be more likely to be unfaithful to her spouse. It is intentional that FGM makes sexual intercourse painful, to ensure that women do not stray. This denial of a woman's right to self-determination is a severe violation of her human rights. It is torture and degradation in the name of "tradition" and "ritual."

FGM hits close to home for me: both of my grandmothers had the external parts of their clitoris removed. It also almost happened to my own mother; thankfully, her mother protected her daughter from other family members. A close friend of mine was mutilated when she was a child; today, she can't feel any sexual pleasure. Although intercourse is extremely painful for her, she feels pressured to go through with it when she is with someone she loves. Every time the subject comes up, my friend bursts into tears.

Knowing that women across the world continue to be subjected to this torture makes me sick to my stomach. This is why I use my voice to lift up those who are harmed by FGM and to inspire the eradication of this injustice once and for all.

Women have the right to health, security, and physical integrity. We have the right to be free from torture, including cruel and degrading treatment such as female genital mutilation (FGM). We have the right to enjoy our sexuality, to be free from pain, and to live without the trauma that FGM continues to perpetuate.

Breast Flattening

Breast flattening is another degrading practice that impacts women's bodily and psychological integrity. During this process, pubescent girls' breasts are ironed, massaged, flattened, and/or pounded down over a period of time (sometimes years) to delay their development or to make their breasts disappear entirely. Breast flattening is meant to prevent rape by making teenage girls look less "womanly"—despite the fact that the only person who is responsible for a rape is the one who commits it. Ironically, breast flattening is often performed by members of the girl's family, who believe they are protecting the girl from abuse—but they don't stop to consider that they themselves are the abusers. It is a selfish response to a girl's budding sexuality, as it is focused less on protecting the girl than on protecting the family's "honor," which would be called into question if the girl had sexual relations outside of marriage.

I heard about breast flattening for the first time when I was ten years old and just starting to develop. I constantly complained about my breasts, which were tender and caused me a lot of pain. One day, one of my aunts told me, "I can help you make them disappear if they annoy you that much." Curious, I asked her how she could do this.

Her response shocked me: she informed me that she would use the spatula we used to make *placali* (a cassava paste boiled in water) to pound my breasts until they were flat. I was aghast. My breasts already hurt—why would I want someone to pound them down with a spatula?!

I gave her an emphatic no, which made her laugh. It still disturbs me that she was so casual about suggesting this act of violence. She said, "You and your mom are too modern. You're not supposed to grow breasts at this age. Don't let boys approach you because of your breasts. Boys are not good." I realized that my aunt was accustomed to this practice, and that many girls my age were still being subjected to it as a way to keep them "safe."

Sometimes, abuse can come under the guise of "protection." Our educational system must stop teaching young girls how to protect themselves; instead, it must teach young boys how to conduct themselves. Women should not be held accountable for the suffering that is inflicted upon us by others!

Child Marriage

Child marriage occurs in every region of the world and is practiced across cultures, religions, and ethnicities. The highest rates of child marriage by country are observed in sub-Saharan Africa. Child marriage generally refers to marriages that take place before age eighteen, but for many girls, marriage occurs much earlier. In some countries, girls as young as seven or eight are forced by their families to marry much older men.

The reasons are diverse. Parents sometimes believe that they are increasing their family's economic opportunities. However, child marriage exposes girls to physical and mental health problems and violence, and it perpetuates a cycle of sex-based inequality. Marriage effectively ends a girl's childhood, deprives her of education, minimizes her economic opportunities, increases her risk of domestic violence, and puts her at risk for early, frequent, and very high-risk pregnancies.

In November 2020, in Ivory Coast, a fourteen-year-old girl killed her husband because she was tired of the constant rape and violence. She was fortunate that some women's rights associations advocated on her behalf so that she wouldn't be convicted of a crime and placed in prison. Countless other young girls in my country take matters into their own hands by killing themselves a few months after being married by force. Although child marriage is illegal, our government does not do enough to actively fight it. Girls here and around the world deserve to live full childhoods, to go to school, to be free of the violence and negative health consequences associated with child marriage, and to choose for themselves and without violence or coercion when, whom, and if they will marry.

Domestic Violence and Femicide

Domestic violence is any abuse (physical, mental, or otherwise) that a person commits against someone they are intimately involved with, most often in a romantic relationship. Across the world, women are more affected by domestic violence. They also tend to experience more severe forms of domestic violence, and many cases end tragically in the death of the victim.

Feminists in my country are doing their best to raise awareness around this topic, and while attitudes are slowly shifting, we are far from where we need to be. Many times, if a woman attempts to leave a violent partner, people express surprise. The popular opinion is that a good woman is supposed to correct her own behaviors that make the man beat her. She is also supposed to pray to God to help her husband change. If she attempts to hold him accountable, people will demonize her and turn her husband into the victim; exposing a perpetrator is seen as destroying his life. My mother's younger sister has been a victim of domestic violence. She was married at the age of seventeen to a man who was very brutal. She had a daughter with him and endured a great deal in that marriage. She was his second wife, and both she and the first wife were mentally and physically abused. If her husband had a bad day, he took his frustrations out on them. He beat and insulted them for the smallest "mistakes." For example, if meals weren't cooked on time, he might yell at, slap, shake, or kick my aunt.

Sometimes, these acts of violence crossed the line into burnings, strangulation attempts, and beatings with sharp or dangerous objects. He attempted to starve my aunt. Even when she was pregnant, he did not stop the violence. She endured his abuse for many years before she decided to leave him. She had no work or money, but she finally summoned the courage to end that horrible marriage.

My aunt stayed at our home with her daughter for a year before she left to be with another man. I was shocked to discover the extent of the abuse she had endured. I'd grown up with a mother who had made it perfectly clear that abuse was not OK and that I should never accept that kind of behavior from a man or anyone else. Unfortunately, as I recognized, many women—including my aunt and perhaps even

Being afraid of your partner or having them humiliate you, yell at you, put you down, blame you for their bad behavior, treat you as their personal property, control your life, and make you feel you aren't good enough is not normal—it is toxic.

We tend to diminish emotional abuse, but it often leads to physical abuse and, in some tragic instances, death. It is very important to recognize the signs. Remember that someone who abuses you will never stop. Their excuses and apologies are methods that test how far they can take their manipulation. One instance of abuse is already one instance too many—when it happens, it's time to leave. If you are pressured to stay with threats, don't hesitate to seek help and talk to your loved ones.

her young daughter—have been raised to normalize violence and to believe they deserve abuse because they don't act "right."

Some of my friends insist that if a boyfriend apologizes after slapping you, he should be forgiven. I once asked a friend why she would stay with someone who treated her so poorly, and she explained: "He treats me like that because he is jealous. He is jealous because he loves me. Also, he's sorry for what he did, and I'm not completely innocent either, so I understand his reaction." When I tried to convince her to leave that dangerous situation, she accused me of wanting to destroy her relationship and stopped talking to me altogether.

If a woman grows up experiencing violence from men in her family, she may become conditioned to believe that this is how things are and should be. Jealousy, rage, and other toxic behaviors are seen as signs of love rather than as dysfunctional and disempowering acts. I once heard an old woman say that a man who never beats his wife doesn't love her; it may sound shocking, but there are many people who agree with this sentiment. Feminists and other activists are working to change this deeply rooted mentality, but it often feels like an uphill battle, as women continue to die under the fists of their partners on a daily basis.

Obstetric Violence

Obstetric violence comprises all forms of physical or mental abuse, mistreatment, or disrespect a woman might experience during labor and delivery at the hands of hospital staff.

I have no children myself, but many women close to me have spoken of their terrible pregnancy experiences. Women with the least money and other resources are the ones who suffer the most. Because delivery in private hospitals tends to be expensive and therefore reserved for only the most privileged, there is less chance of mistreatment. However, in public hospitals, women undergo a great deal of trauma from medical personnel.

Many women endure physical and mental violence from midwives in public hospitals, who are known for insulting, yelling at, and sometimes even hitting women during labor. If a woman screams loudly, medical staff might get annoyed and offer highly inappropriate comments such as "When you was fucking, it was good, right? Now it's time to take the

Giving birth can be a traumatic experience; a woman needs to be in stable and supportive conditions. She needs love, patience, and professionalism from medical staff before, during, and after the delivery of her child.

consequences, so shut up and push," or "Stop screaming, bitch." Even if women dare to protest, their entreaties seldom change this horrific treatment. Without money or influence, they find that their complaints fall on closed ears.

This abusive treatment continues during delivery. When my uncle's girlfriend was giving birth to her first child, medical staff performed an episiotomy (a surgical incision to facilitate a quick and easeful delivery) on her without due warning or anesthesia. She was also sewn up without anesthesia. In Ivory Coast, episiotomies occur almost automatically for women giving birth to their first child, even when they are not necessary. Medical personnel justify the procedure by saying that the pain of contractions is so intense that most women won't feel the cut. If a woman can endure the pain of labor, she should be able to endure this additional pain.

I was in the waiting room during her procedure, and to this day, I can still hear her cries of suffering. It was such a devastating experience that she decided not to have any more children. After she went home, one of her stitches broke and she should have returned to the hospital, but her trauma far outweighed her fear of medical complications, and she never went back.

Another common form of obstetrical violence is called the "husband stitch." It is an unnecessary extra stitch given during the repair process after a vaginal birth that is supposed to make the vagina tighter and increase the pleasure of a woman's male sexual partner. It is also often done without the woman's consent or even her knowledge.

The Justice System's Failure to Protect Women

In many parts of the world, laws permit men's violence to go unpunished. Although rape and violence against women may not be legal, women are afforded few protections and are discouraged from even filing charges against their assailants.

Navigating law enforcement can itself be a challenging experience. Often, victims and survivors will be forced to answer questions that retraumatize them and that overtly or covertly place the blame on them. These questions might include "What were you wearing when the guy raped you?" or "What did you do to be beaten?" In some cases, a woman will be asked, "Are you sure you want to destroy this man's life? Why can't you just forgive him?"

In Ivory Coast, even when it's been proved that a crime took place, perpetrators' sentences are usually short. Many men who have been convicted of rape or physically assaulting a woman face less than a year of jail time. And the justice system does not offer protection to a victim once the perpetrator is out of jail, so many men continue to harass or stalk their victims.

A good friend of mine attempted to file a complaint against an abusive ex who continued to threaten and harass her after their breakup. One day, he came to her home and physically assaulted her. As soon as he left, she went to the hospital to create a medical record of her wounds and bruises. But when she went to the police the next day, they interrogated her about why she wanted to destroy the life of a man she'd once loved. One officer assumed that she was lying and that she merely wanted to put her ex in jail because he had broken up with her.

When she insisted on filing the complaint, they gave her a piece of paper that she was supposed to hand-deliver to her ex so that he could come to the station and give his version of the story. The idea that law enforcement officials would expect a woman who was filing a complaint about a man's assault to then approach him demonstrates how dismissive the system is—and just how little it values the safety and well-being of women. My friend was so disheartened that she decided to let the incident go. She simply moved to a new house in the hopes that her ex would never find her. Like many other women, she received a rude awakening: she was truly the only person she could count on to keep herself safe.

Post-Traumatic Stress Disorder and Women's Mental Health

Post-traumatic stress disorder (PTSD) is characterized by the inability to fully recover after experiencing or witnessing a traumatic event. Even minor occurrences—such as hearing a song, seeing a specific image, or encountering an object associated with the traumatic event—might trigger a person's memories to the extent that they feel they are reliving the most difficult moments of their lives. Women who experience violence often deal with unacknowledged PTSD that makes day-to-day living extremely difficult. Their work lives and private lives, including their connection to their bodies and sexuality, can be severely impacted.

I've experienced PTSD in the wake of being a victim of the practice known as stealthing, when a man removes a condom during intercourse without his partner's consent or knowledge. At the time, I wasn't fully educated about sexually transmitted infections, but my mother had always told me to protect myself, so I was always extremely rigorous about using condoms. I told my partners in no uncertain terms that we would either have safe sex or no sex.

One of my partners was clearly not excited about the prospect of using condoms, but he agreed to it. By the end of our first sexual encounter, I realized that he wasn't wearing a condom. I was furious. When I asked him what had happened, he casually informed me that he'd taken it off in the middle of sex because he couldn't feel anything.

I spiraled into a cycle of imagining every possible worst-case scenario. What if he had HIV or AIDS (which at that time, I'd thought was synonymous with death, since I'd received very poor education about the condition)? What if he had transmitted another STI to me in his negligence? I immediately became cold toward him, which seemed to perplex him. I told him that he'd had no right to remove the condom without even talking to me about it. Still, for him, it was no big deal.

I needed to wait three months before getting an HIV test, since it would not be detectable until then. Those three months of waiting were perhaps the worst three months of my life. I was under perpetual stress; whenever I had flashbacks of my sexual encounter

with this man, I felt extremely anxious and the experience of violation came surging back. I confined myself to my room all day, and I had no interest in a social life or anything else. It felt like I had a constant lump in my throat that made it very hard to breathe. If HIV was mentioned on TV or on social media, I felt an intense pain in my chest—so intense that I often believed it would kill me. I had constant nightmares and woke up crying in the middle of the night. I would even faint for no discernible reason.

My mother was worried about my sudden change in behavior, but I feared opening up to her. As much as I loved my mom, I was worried that she'd be disappointed in my choices. But one day, my chest pain became so intense that she sent me to the emergency room. After a thorough examination, my doctor determined that I'd had an anxiety attack. When he left the room, my mom gently inquired as to what had caused such a severe reaction. I burst into tears and told her everything. She immediately took me into her arms and reassured me. A huge burden lifted from my shoulders that day.

The doctor gave me some medication to decrease the intensity of my symptoms, and it helped. Finally, I reached the three-month mark and got my HIV test. It was such a relief to see that my results were negative. I slowly began to improve and my PTSD symptoms dissipated after a couple of weeks. However, the impacts on my body were so intense that they left me sensitized. I occasionally experience anxiety attacks to this day. If you have ever experienced the same thing, I empathize—I know how disruptive and painful it can be. Just know that you are not alone, and that seeking help will only serve to break the stigma of silence and alleviate your suffering.

The Valorization of Female Suffering

Violence against women is so normalized in Ivory Coast that not only do people not condemn it but they tend to see this suffering as a sign of a woman's virtue.

Many people will measure a woman's value and strength on the basis of her ability to take and endure abuse. Women are considered dignified, respectable, and good wife material if they remain silent about their maltreatment. A "real" African woman can accept her husband's infidelity and his violence without speaking about it. A "real" African woman gives birth without using any methods to alleviate her pain. In fact, women who use epidurals or give birth via C-section may be insulted or denigrated by those around them for their "unnatural" choices. Likewise, women who accept modern conveniences such as dishwashers and laundry machines are considered lazy for not doing everything manually.

I am saddened when I meet women who see their ability to endure pain and suffering as a source of pride. It is yet another distortion of our resilience. True resilience is not about suffering—it is about our willingness to recognize that we don't deserve to suffer. True resilience is our ability to honor ourselves and to demonstrate that we are worth more than the poor treatment that society has deemed acceptable. We must work together to create societies in which women don't become unwitting accomplices to their suffering and oppression—but in which we are able to recognize injustice when we see it and to fight to make our voices heard... not just for ourselves but for all our sisters.

So many traumatized women are doing their best to thrive in the face of what they have endured. I want to give all the love I can to these women, including myself, for what they have lived through... for their courage to prevail and to fight for justice... No woman should be expected to shoulder the burden of living in and challenging patriarchy at the expense of her own mental health.

**May we all be free from suffering.
May we know and live our wholeness
in every moment.**

SELF-LOVE

My feminist activism continues to play a huge role in improving my life and increasing my self-esteem. My previous views were dominated by internalized sexism and White supremacy, but feminism gave me the language to deconstruct these beliefs and to claim my own agency. It helped me to live my life for myself instead of trying to conform to social norms and other people's expectations.

As I explored feminism, I began to understand how patriarchy destroys women from within and installs negative beliefs, like "I'm not good enough if I don't look a certain way"; "I'm not valuable if I'm not married or a mother"; "It's not realistic to do that activity because I'm a woman"—all of these become the air we breathe and the water we unknowingly drink.

For me, feminism overturned these ideas so that I could see them as the lies they really are. My feminism has empowered me by revealing that I am perfectly capable of adopting any role I want to. I deserve to take up space and to live my life in the ways that I deem best. My opinions are valid. I am worthy and beautiful, no matter what I look like. I deserve to do whatever I can to nurture my potential and to achieve my dreams.

For me, the goal of feminism is to free women and give them more choices. If a woman decides that she is OK with traditional sex roles, I don't think it's useful to judge her or to regard her as weak or brainwashed. While we may not agree with her choices, there is no one way to be a woman in this world, and we are not fighting to impose a new normal—but to empower women to consciously choose the life they want.

While my life has not always been easy, feminism has offered me a framework that builds my resilience and makes me remember who I really am—beyond what society has told me. It gives me the self-awareness and confidence to embrace all parts of myself: my body, my biology, my sexuality, my life experiences and opinions, my choices, and my dreams. It brings me closer to joy and to living a life that is true to myself.

Recovering from My Eating Disorder

Body dysmorphia and poor body image are important topics to me, as I am recovering from the harmful effects of bulimia and anorexia.

It started when I was thirteen. I was already in high school because I had skipped a grade due to my good marks in school. The other girls in my class were older and looked like "real women," according to my country's standards of female beauty: thick, with curves, large breasts, a big butt, and light skin.

I was the complete opposite: a slender girl with dark skin. It was very frustrating for me, because I wanted to feel attractive. I was envious of the girls in my class who had bodies that clearly drew the interest of boys. I couldn't change being dark-skinned, since my mom didn't allow me to use bleaching products. However, I believed I could overcome my skinniness by eating more.

In Ivory Coast, on top of skin-bleaching products, women use creams, injections, and other products to make their butts and breasts look bigger. Much like skin bleaching, some of these techniques are extremely dangerous and nonsensical. Some women here even use Maggi Savor, a popular liquid seasoning for cooking, as an enema—which is rumored to give the user a bigger butt.

I knew enough to avoid such unsafe methods, but eating more felt like a less dangerous option. I started to binge on the unhealthiest foods. I quickly gained weight, which made me feel proud. As I became thicker, my confidence grew, too. I was receiving more compliments, which felt affirming.

However, something else began to happen: I was eating ravenously, even when I wasn't hungry. Sometimes, my stomach was so full that I literally felt sick. I ate like this for nine months. I even had to get a new school uniform because the old one became too tight. I hadn't taken into account that I couldn't simply eat my way into larger breasts and butt—my belly was also substantially bigger. This didn't bother me that much... until a boy in my class made a nasty joke about my belly in front of all my other classmates—including a boy I had a huge crush on.

The whole class, including my crush, started laughing. I was a young girl seeking validation, and this experience shook me to my core.

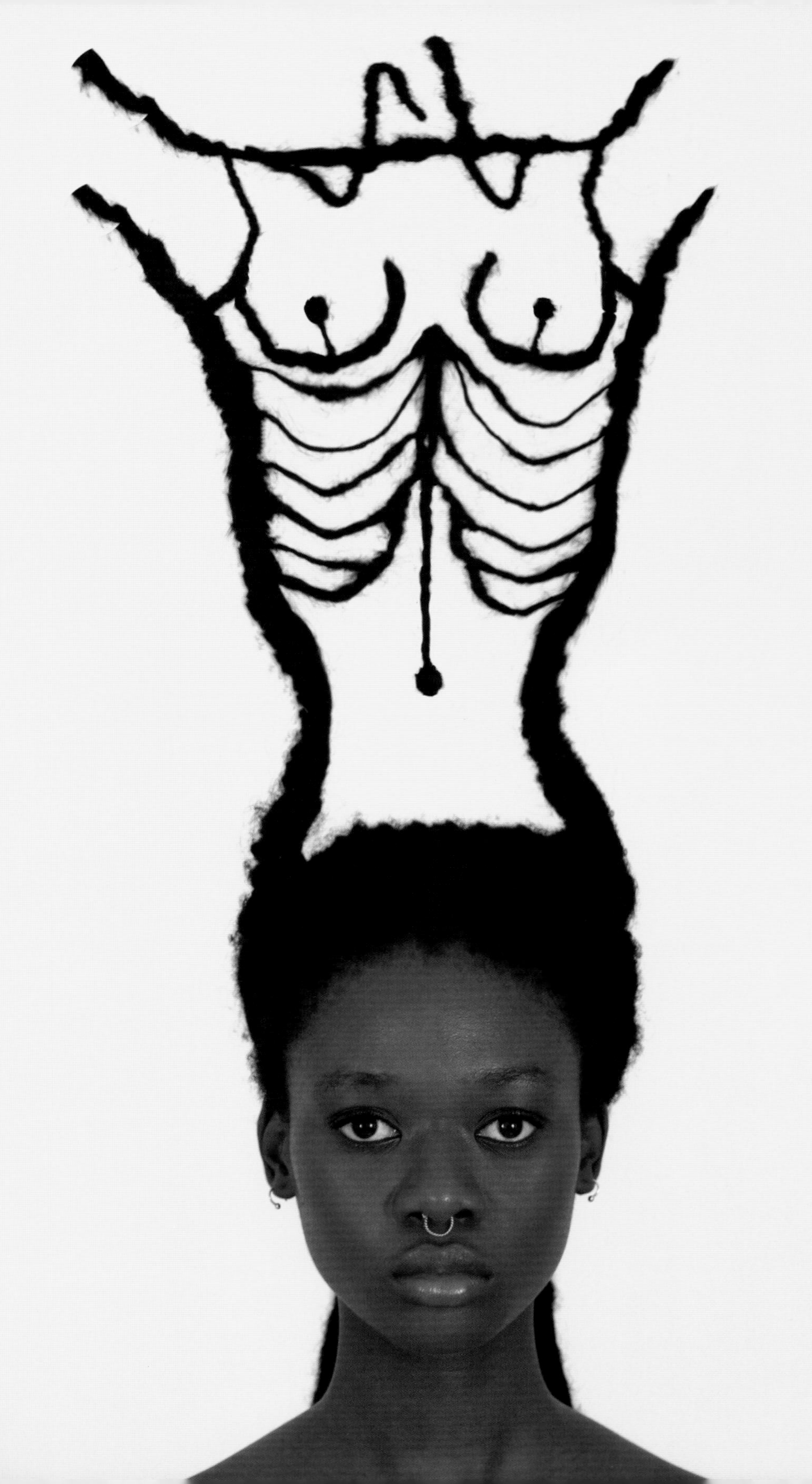

To this day, I don't know how I mustered the strength to hold in my tears in front of everyone. Instead of eating dinner when I went home, I skipped a meal. This was the beginning of my anorexia.

Abruptly, with no transition, I started to obsess over every inch of fat on my body. What had made me feel beautiful a couple of days earlier became something I hated because of an offhand remark. I was determined at all cost to lose what I'd fought to gain.

I became paranoid about food and started eating less and less every day, starving myself until I constantly felt weak and foggy. Every time I thought I was at my end and needed to nourish myself, that memory of being a laughingstock due to my big belly came surging back.

Sometimes, my hunger was so painful that I broke down and stuffed myself with food. It was the most awful feeling...and that was how I started to vomit intentionally. Bulimia became my chosen tactic, as I realized I could eat everything I wanted...and then I could simply throw it all up.

In about three months, I lost all the weight I'd gained over nine months. My mom was understandably concerned and even took me to see a doctor—but I assured her that I was fine.

More time passed, and I lost even more weight. My belly became flat once more, and I returned to my original skinny state...but my fear of food hadn't disappeared. I drank a lot of water to avoid being hungry. I smelled and chewed my food so I could savor the taste without swallowing it. And if I ended up swallowing, I would throw up minutes later.

After a few months, I was so extremely skinny that my bones were visible. I wore baggy clothing to avoid my mother's worried attention. Gradually, my period stopped altogether. I felt cold and tired. I was able to maintain good grades at school, but I was empty inside.

My whole life revolved around how to avoid eating. Sometimes, I prayed to God to help me feel better. I attempted to find some way to resolve what felt like a hopeless situation. I started to eat a little more and tried to keep myself from throwing up...but as soon as I would gain a little weight, I would become terrified about regaining my belly and attracting even more mockery. Thus, the cycle of binging, vomiting, and skipping meals repeated itself.

On so many occasions, I tried to stop because I knew this behavior was hurting me...but every time, I failed. This lasted for about three years. My mom attempted to talk to me so she could understand what I was going through. Almost everyone around me was worried about my mental and physical health. Even with my oversized clothes, I looked sickly and unhealthy.

My breaking point came when I was in my bedroom, changing my clothes, and my mom came into the room without knocking. When she got a glimpse of my naked body, she screamed and burst into tears. She begged me to start eating again. She said she was afraid she would lose me.

Witnessing her shock motivated a real desire to recover. It wasn't easy—I experienced many challenges and much soul searching—but just as the memory of the boy making fun of me had been the catalyst for my eating disorders, the thought of my mother's tears and the pain in her eyes as she shared her deepest fears with me was enough to keep me on the long and hard journey to recovery and wholeness. Of course, this is a journey that does not need to be traveled alone; if you or someone you know is facing an eating disorder, there is help available in the form of therapists, support groups, and people who have journeyed the same roads as you. Please seek help if you need it.

Welcoming My Periods

One of the most stigmatized processes of a woman's body is menstruation. In a lot of cultures, including that of Ivory Coast, menstrual blood is considered dirty and disgusting. In some parts of the world, women on their periods are expected to leave their village altogether and to isolate themselves in huts. In other parts of the world, women on their periods are expected to avoid activities such as cooking or going to school. Periods are typically associated with impurity, and it isn't unusual for people to refer to menstruation as a "curse."

Even in parts of the world that are considered modern and advanced, people rarely talk about menstruation, even though 50 percent of the population bleeds. The avoidance of the topic is obvious in advertisements for period products, wherein blue liquid is used to simulate menstrual blood—which is strange, considering the amount of violence, blood, and gore that we encounter on a daily basis in popular entertainment.

I've been through my own journey toward acceptance of menstruation. I recall being in high school one day when my period came early, so I was not prepared with tampons or pads. I improvised by going to the bathroom and folding a large piece of toilet paper to put in my underpants. Two hours later, when I got up from my seat at the end of class, my entire skirt was soaked in blood: the toilet paper had not been sufficient protection, since I experience a heavy flow in the first days of my period.

It was only when a male classmate said in a mocking voice, "Ky, did you poop on yourself?" that I realized in horror what had happened. The whole class started laughing, and a girl replied, "Are you stupid? It's not poop—it's her period." The boy responded, "It's all the same to me! Pussy diarrhea! I'm sure if I get close, it will be stinky." By this point, some girls in the class were also laughing. I was frozen and couldn't say anything. It was so humiliating that I avoided going to school the next day.

To my period: you have made my life difficult at times, and I've experienced you in the context of a society that perceives you as nasty, dirty, and impure. But I love you and I am grateful for you. You are natural, and you are here each month to remind me that my body is in perfect working order.

To all the women who suffer from painful periods, endometriosis, and other difficulties around their menstruation: you are loved and seen. I wish for you never to have to suffer in silence, but for the support of your sisters to lift you up in shared recognition and empathy.

On countless occasions, I've blamed my body and my female biology for my unhappiness. I hated having a period. I hated having breasts. Sometimes, I even hated features that were considered beautiful, when they garnered unwanted attention. But if there's one thing I know today, it's that shame and humiliation should not be women's burden to carry. This shame is just another way for patriarchy to exert control over us.

In truth, women's bodies are beautiful and amazing—works of pure art. Our bodies are the matrix of humanity. Our periods are a blessing—intricately timed natural rhythms that somehow manage to follow the cycle of the moon. While I myself don't wish to have children, I honor the childbearing capacity of my body.

Body Hair Is Natural!

Beauty standards the world over involve false ideas of femininity versus masculinity. And no matter how liberated a woman is, one area that is likely to bring up feelings of insecurity or shame is her amount of body hair.

Hair on a woman's body is stigmatized in most societies. Women who dare to embrace body hair are often insulted or even attacked. Media, which tends to embrace the standard of hairless, perfectly smooth skin, doesn't help matters. Prevailing beauty standards negate the fact that what is considered "normal" isn't actually the norm, but a fabrication.

I started growing armpit hair around the age of eleven. At first, I was happy because it made me feel like I was maturing. Arm lifted in pride, I would gaze at my hair in a mirror. However, I understood that I was expected to shave my armpits. I hated the routine: my skin became hypersensitive, and shaving sometimes resulted in lesions and redness. I tried to minimize the effects by shaving only once a month or so.

One day, at the age of fifteen, I posted a photograph of myself on social media without realizing my armpit hair was visible in the photo. Needless to say, I received a number of brutal comments—some from people I knew and some from ones I didn't. Comments like "This is dirty," "You're disgusting," and "I can buy you a razor if you want." I quickly deleted the picture and shaved that same day. After that episode, I began shaving more regularly. I still hated it, but it wasn't as bad as the derogatory comments I'd received, which shattered my pride in myself.

It took me years to learn how to be confident and to see myself as beautiful without shaving. Even now, when I post a picture in which my armpits are visible, I receive violent comments and messages. Sometimes, it crosses a line and I receive rape threats. It never ceases to astonish me that so many people are invested in outmoded beauty standards and that they can't stomach a woman who is strong enough to move beyond them.

It always amazes me when people justify their disdain for armpit hair with rationalizations such as "It's unhygienic!" As humans, we have hair all over our bodies. Our hair has a natural function, just like every other part of our body. It is there to protect our skin, regulate our sweat, and prevent skin-to-skin contact, which can create chafing and irritation.

I also commonly hear "It's just not for women." But if that were the case, why do all women naturally grow armpit hair? Most of us find it difficult to accept that our likes and dislikes are largely manipulated and shaped by society and by capitalism, so we find ways to justify our perspectives. But before we come up with knee-jerk rationalizations, we must question our conditioning and do our research.

In recent years, the removal of pubic hair has become the social norm for women across the world. I prefer not to shave mine, because nature put it there for a reason! In fact, most obstetricians and gynecologists don't recommend removing pubic hair, as it protects this delicate part of our bodies from bacteria and other harmful pathogens. I believe the widespread obsession with youth is connected to the preference for a hairless pubic region, which I find disturbing and infantilizing. I celebrate my pubic hair, because it reminds me that I am a grown woman.

Saying Yes to Aging

Aging can create huge insecurity in women. Many consider asking a woman her age to be disrespectful, and it's considered a compliment to insist that a woman looks years younger than her age. Sometimes, I surprise myself when I recognize that I'm afraid of growing old: one day, I tried an "aging" filter on one of my photographs, and I was terrified by the result.

Our beauty products come with phrases like "anti-aging" or "Turn back the clock," suggesting that a woman's beauty disappears as she ages. But this is simply not true. A different type of beauty emerges: a beauty that reveals our experiences, our fights, our trials, our victories, and our wisdom with every wrinkle and laugh line. A beauty that reveals everything we've learned—which can lead us to embrace a more authentic joy and sense of self than we had when we were younger and perhaps more concerned about others' opinions of us. Some of the most beautiful women I've encountered are older, and their beauty radiates from them like a unique light.

A human being is supposed to evolve physically and mentally, so in many ways, it is a blessing and a privilege to reveal our age. Aging is not a disease that should be treated, fixed, erased, or hidden. I know for myself that I am no longer afraid to grow old, because I fully understand that beauty is ageless.

Embracing Physical Differences

In a world ruled by norms and standards, it can feel very difficult to be physically different. People with visible disabilities are often forced to endure stares, mockery, inappropriate questions, and insulting comments. And many differences in a woman's body—from skin conditions like acne or eczema to hirsutism (excess body hair) and alopecia (hair loss)—can impact a woman's self-esteem.

But our physical differences can be our superpowers. In a world where everyone is trying to look the same, we can embrace the power of fully accepting ourselves and our differences. We can use our differences to educate, inspire, empower, and advocate. So, please...be proud and own the things that make you different!

Transforming My "Flaws" into Beauty

I used to hate smiling because I didn't like how it made my nose widen. I felt that my nose was already too large when my face was relaxed, so I hated how prominent it became when my face was more expressive.

This insecurity about my nose started when I was very little. I had an aunt who used to comment that I had clearly taken after my father, since I had his big nose. Every time she visited, she would make remarks about my nose. She intended these to be innocent jokes that would make people laugh, but they made me fixate on my nose as a "flaw."

I prayed that one day I would have enough money to get nose-reduction surgery. I often pinched my nose, hoping this would make it thinner. Of course, it didn't change—and even worse, I would give myself painful bruises. I burst into tears quite a few times in front of the mirror. The lack of representation of Black women in the media didn't help, either. Those who were considered beautiful were often those with small, European-seeming features.

I have come such a long way since then. Today, I love the photographs in which I am smiling, and I am happy to have my unique face: I love my large, expressive nose, my gorgeous, full lips, and my strong, magnetic eyes. I am deeply in love with my features and the story they tell about me—and I long for other women to feel the same way. Every time I see a non-White woman who has gotten a nose job, I feel heartbroken that society tricked her into believing her original nose wasn't good enough.

Society has taken aspects of our bodies that are quite normal and expected and turned them into anomalies and flaws, demanding a constant search for "perfection." Television, film, magazines, and social media present glamorous images of women that are carefully erased, retouched, and Photoshopped to conveniently blot out the "imperfections." People, especially young girls, tend to believe they are abnormal in comparison.

I myself have prominent dark circles under my eyes, and I actually love the depth and dimension they add to my eyes. I also have cellulite and stretch marks, despite being skinny, and I appreciate that this makes me unique. I have some scars here and there, which stand as powerful reminders of everything I've been through. I also have acne, hyperpigmentation, large pores, and oily skin.

At a certain point in my life, I did everything I could to erase these features. I can't recall how many times I cursed my reflection due to a pimple, or frowned at my breasts because of the chicken pox scars they held, or attempted to rub my stretch marks away, or worked out obsessively to eradicate my cellulite.

But none of this takes away from my beauty. I recall posting a close-up picture of myself without makeup on Instagram, taken with a professional camera to make every "flaw" visible. A painter sent me a message saying that all the marks made my face more interesting to draw. It was such a beautiful compliment.

Today, I have a better and kinder view of my body. I work out for my health, and I don't hold unrealistic expectations when I use makeup. I honor the marks on my body because they are a sign that I am a normal and naturally resilient human being. I reject the desire to erase every texture, every line, every mark. We are not dolls or drawings. Behind every scar, every mark—every sign of transformation that is written on our body—is a beautiful story.

Stretch marks are beautiful. They are powerful tributaries on the map of our body, reminding us of the important landmarks and paths we've taken that have made us who we are.

Gap teeth are beautiful. In many cultures, this "imperfection" is a sign of good luck.

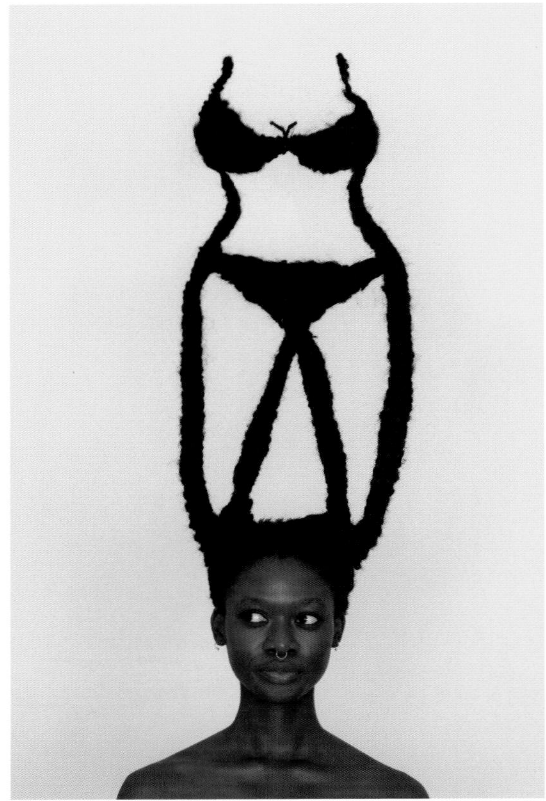

All body shapes are beautiful. Our bodies are the vehicles for our souls, and each body has its own story to tell.

Whether small, large, pendulous, round, conical, bell-shaped, or marbled with stretch marks, our breasts are all markers of our unique beauty.

The diversity of our bodies is integral to the recognition of true beauty. Beauty standards don't do justice to the broad array of possibilities that manifest in our bodies. It is your uniqueness that makes you gorgeous, so embrace it!

Your scars tell a powerful story about your wounds, your healing, and your resilience.

Nothing on your body is too big or too small. Everything is just the perfect size.

A Woman's Sexuality Is Her Own

What could be more natural than our sexuality, which gives us pleasure, creates intimacy with ourselves and others, and has the power to bring forth life?

Sadly, patriarchy has exerted so much control over women's bodies that many of us can't see our sexuality as a natural part of who we are. Society attempts to own women's sexuality and capacity for pleasure—very likely because controlling this force of nature is yet another way of limiting our freedom. Sometimes, this control is obvious and explicit, such as in places where premarital or extramarital sex is punishable by death; sometimes it is implicit, such as in cultures where persistent slut-shaming is used to police women's sexual behavior.

I had my first orgasm at the age of six, by accident. Of course, I didn't know what had just happened to me! But after I made that discovery, I began touching myself regularly. Embracing my sexuality was an uphill battle for me in my early years. Because of internalized misogyny, I felt shame and disgust around my desires. I used to hate myself after masturbating. Sometimes, I even asked God to help me stop. I'd grown up hearing that women who masturbated were cursed and had let demons enter their lives and souls. I recognized that men were not demonized for doing the same thing; rather, their behavior was seen as natural.

Only at around the age of eighteen did I begin to see self-pleasuring as a way of exploring my own body, of learning what I like and don't like, and of improving sexual communication with a partner. I actively started to recognize that women have the intrinsic right to pleasure. Our clitoris is the only human organ with pleasure as its sole function—so if we aren't supposed to feel pleasure, why is it there to begin with?

The desire to play with and enjoy our sexuality is a basic human need. It is important that women be free to love who they want to love (men or women), free to enjoy their sexuality the way they want, free to have zero or one or multiple sexual partners, free to speak about it, and even free to monetize it if they wish. I understand that sex work is a delicate and controversial topic in the feminist community. Some believe that sex work exploits women's bodies and contributes to sexualization and violence against women. I agree with this because I recognize that most women who engage in sex work don't do it of their own free will, and many women suffer not only at the hands of their clients but also from punitive forms of law enforcement. And sex work can have a lot of repercussions for women who don't even engage in the industry. However, I can't judge another woman for her personal circumstances and choices. What is most important to me is that all women are able to live their lives free and unharmed.

A woman's body is made to feel pleasure. Sexuality is a natural part of the human experience, and it is important that women learn to explore their bodies and sexual desires without shame or guilt. All women deserve to engage in safe, consensual sexual activities. All women deserve complete autonomy when it comes to how they wish to relate to and express their own sexuality.

Our Opinion, Our Voice

Not only are women judged for our physical appearance, we are also judged for merely possessing an opinion. In every sphere, from politics to the entertainment industry, women are infantilized, ridiculed, minimized, and dismissed. And if we hold tight to our ideals, we are often placed under a harsh magnifying glass. In Ivory Coast, feminists are seen as contemptible, destined to die alone and embittered. Although I know a lot of women who believe in the equality of the sexes, they are often afraid to call themselves a "feminist."

Women's religious beliefs and choices seem to place them on the hot seat more often than men. For example, in some parts of the world, Muslim women are the victims of harassment by people who perceive their religion to be oppressive and consider them to be brainwashed. In Ivory Coast, this is not an issue, but women who are atheists or nonreligious face the same kind of scrutiny. When I explain to people that I am not religious because many religions justify women's subordination to men, they look upon me with horror and disbelief. But I believe that religion is a personal choice and that no one should impose their belief systems upon us.

One of the most personal choices a woman can make—her choice of partner—is also often mocked and called into question. Women with high standards for dating are considered materialistic and lazy—as are those with specific physical preferences. Or if women insist on loyalty and fidelity, they might be treated like spoiled princesses who need to be taken down a peg. Many seem to believe that women should simply be grateful for whatever they get rather than asking for the very best. In fact, women who truly love themselves *should* create dating criteria that will make them happy. As for the rest of us, it's none of our business!

I have previously written about having been severely shamed as selfish and unfeminine for not wanting marriage or children—by friends, strangers, and people online. No matter what you accomplish in your life, if you are an African woman who has not married or had lots of children, you are seen as unworthy and incomplete. In Ivory Coast, many notable women who are public figures are shamed if they've reached a certain age and are not yet married. However, in other parts of the world, if a woman's main goal is to marry and have a family, she might be perceived as stupid or not ambitious enough. It seems that no matter what women decide, we can never win.

But a woman's personal decisions, however she has arrived at them, should be respected; we should never have to justify how we choose to live.

Freeing Ourselves from the Pain of Judgment

As a feminist, I've learned to recognize that while society might prefer for me to stay quiet and compliant, my voice counts. I can use it to create transformation, spread awareness about important social topics, and stand up for myself. I can use it to express my truth and to shape my reality.

Unfortunately, a woman's expression of honesty is too often distorted by society. She might be deemed a "bitch," or "dangerous," or "unfeminine." We witness character-assassination campaigns, particularly against women occupying a place in the public eye—especially now that social media has become such a huge forum for naysayers and haters.

I have experienced the pain and humiliation of being a target simply for being myself. But my conscience is light because I know that at every moment, I am being true to myself and my values. By embracing our opinions and being courageous in expressing them, we gain an incredible power that inspires others to achieve great things and change the world for the better.

Howl with all your strength what is inside your heart. The world needs to hear your voice.

Women may shy away from expressing their opinions because of the toxic phenomenon known as "cancel culture." Famous figures are most often touched by it, but everyone is subject to it. Cancel culture entails boycotting people and brands over behavior or speech that might be considered offensive. While speaking out against injustice is important, cancel culture can result in a mob mentality that foregoes true accountability in favor of punishment. This harsh form of judgment can cause people to lose their jobs, reputations, and livelihoods, or to face tremendous hate and even fatal threats—simply for voicing an unpopular opinion or because the social media police have dredged up something they did in their past.

Cancel culture is often much harsher toward women than men: think about the "controversy" of Justin Timberlake and Janet Jackson's performance at the 2004 Super Bowl halftime show. Timberlake exposed Jackson's nipple but went on to achieve more success in his career, while Jackson was derided for pulling what people called a "publicity stunt" and was blacklisted in the entertainment industry. Talk about double standards!

Cancel culture metes out punishments that are disproportionate to the supposed crime. We encourage free speech but ostracize those who reveal a viewpoint that is not seen as acceptable or progressive—shutting down all critical discussion. If you don't agree with someone, it is natural to take some distance or to stop consuming what this person has produced. But encouraging others to shun the person because you consider her opinion offensive isn't right. Different viewpoints may seem toxic, but so is a lack of tolerance. Nobody should fear cancellation simply for expressing themselves.

Dealing with Online Hate

While online activism can open up discussion on myriad important social issues and spark dialogue between people who are literally oceans apart, it can also open the door to backlash, hate, and bullying.

Cyberbullies aim to annoy, upset, or confuse their targets. The cyberbully hopes for a response as an excuse to agitate their victim further, so it's best not to give them what they want. Of course, ignoring asinine or violent statements is easier said than done; I'm an emotional person, and when someone attacks me, I can respond impulsively. But I've learned that engaging in discussion with bullies is fruitless. They aren't looking to understand you; they are looking to tear you down.

If you're overwhelmed by cyberbullying, take some time away from social media to calm down and feel better. Reporting and blocking your haters is a good way to maintain sanity in such situations. Make screenshots of the hateful messages before they are deleted if the person who has attacked you is not anonymous. This can help you to obtain justice; after all, not everything deserves to be ignored.

What has helped me over time is the constant reminder that other people's words and actions will never define me. Remember that the hate people give for free is most often the very hate they feel for themselves.

What I Do to Feel More Confident

People often ask me, "How did you get to be so confident?" And it's true that I have found a deep and genuine self-love that allows me to project my authentic self out into the world. However, being confident isn't something that's achieved overnight.

As I've shared throughout this book, I've encountered my own dark nights of the soul...times when I felt uncertain and alone, when I was uncomfortable in my own skin and longed to inhabit someone else's. I went through a lot before I came to the realization that true happiness is only possible with self-love, a love that is about unconditional acceptance of one's experience. This includes the so-called flaws, scars, and difficulties that have marked one's path.

Everyone's journey is unique; there is no secret formula. For some, self-confidence can happen instantaneously, sometimes in the wake of a major event that changes that person's self-perception. For others, it's a more gradual awakening...a sense of growing into one's true self over time.

And guess what? Even when you reach the point at which you consider yourself confident, you will constantly be tested by the world! We must all sit with the reality that while many of us aspire to confidence, we live in a society that persistently chips away at our confidence...that casts stones of envy and hatred at strong women.

It is perfectly natural to experience insecurity and doubt. If you are reading this and are not at the point at which you can truly call yourself confident, I want you to know you've got this! You will have ups and downs in your journey, but as long as you continue to shine the light that lives within you—wherever you find yourself, whether it's at a peak or in a valley—you will be fine.

There are lots of tools I've used to keep my own confidence high, and I want to share them with you in the hope that you'll find them useful and uplifting.

Change Your Focus

Too often, we focus on the things we don't like about ourselves. Even if we are OK with a hundred things about ourselves, the negative bias of the mind makes us focus on the two things we consider "not good enough." So we have to teach ourselves how to focus on the positive by shifting our attention and mindset to gratitude and appreciation for all our wonderful qualities. We have a lot more control over our feelings than we give ourselves credit for!

Instead of scrutinizing your pimples, scars, or stretch marks, can you shift your attention to your shiny hair, your beautiful smile, or the other qualities that make you uniquely radiant? Whatever you appreciate about yourself, bring your intentional focus to those things. Over time, this will make you feel much better and more confident about your full self.

This doesn't mean you shouldn't try to improve yourself, but seeking change with a grateful and positive mindset will always be more efficient than doing it with an attitude of self-hatred or negativity.

Words of Affirmation

Our unconscious mind is extremely powerful—and when we work to access it, we begin to change not just our thoughts but also our behavior and habits in the world. One way we can do this is to transform our internal dialogue and intentionally refocus our thoughts to positive affirmations. I know from experience that we can use our conscious activity to shape and change what lives in our unconscious—that place that holds a sea of memories, conditioned responses and reactions, and internalized beliefs that we may not even realize are lurking below the surface.

It is possible to evolve into a place of genuine self-love by affirming to ourselves the thoughts that we would like to be thinking—even if these thoughts feel foreign or unfamiliar at first. I suggest talking to yourself using only appreciative and positive words; eliminate phrases like "I am ugly," "I can't do this," "I'm not good enough," and "I can never get it right." Every day, speak loving words to yourself, such as: "I am beautiful," "I am able to accomplish everything I want to," "I am worthy," "I am strong," and "I trust that my life is moving in the right direction."

The trick is that even if you don't believe what you're saying, keep saying it! Over time, through repetition, the unconscious mind comes to assimilate these new ideas and beliefs and to treat them as reality. Implant positive and gentle thoughts—the kind you would speak to a loved one or a small child—in your own mind. You will eventually wholeheartedly believe these words. Your mind will always accept what you tell it, so learn to tell it good things.

I CAN

Examine Your Relationships

Insecurities can be contagious, but so can confidence. I've been deeply inspired by the many confident people I've met in my life. My hope is that I will in the same way "contaminate" you with my own confidence!

Just as it is important to surround ourselves with uplifting, positive, confident influences who reflect our own brilliance back to us, it's crucial to recognize negative influences who might be poisoning our thoughts and casting doubt on our better qualities. If someone in your life makes you feel bad about yourself, I encourage you to minimize your connection with them and to build yourself up by seeking closer relationships with people who recognize your beauty and worth.

Changing these relationships isn't always easy. The people at the base of our insecurities might be our own parents or perhaps a spouse or partner. It is not always desirable to cut off our loved ones, but it's important to set boundaries and to be honest about the impact others have on us. We can be clear about the consequences of ill treatment on our mental health. And if the people surrounding us have no desire to uplift us, even after we share our truth with them, we need to question our decision to keep them in our lives. People who drain us of our energy and our innate light do not deserve a special place in our hearts.

This is also true for the people we follow on social media. Give yourself permission to unfollow anyone who doesn't make you feel good about yourself. You might love their work, but if you find yourself drowning in a sea of constant negative comparisons, it isn't worth it to keep following them. Nourish yourself with social media that promotes body positivity, that brings out your passions and inspires you to live freely and truthfully, and that helps you celebrate your own positive qualities.

In both the virtual and real worlds, surround yourself with positive people who make you feel good about yourself. It is said that we are the average of the five people we spend the most time with. Do those people kindle a fire in your heart that warms you and others? Make an effort to connect with people who help you realize your magnificent potential—and do the same for them.

Be Kind

The way we act toward other people is often more a reflection of who we are than of who they are. What we believe about ourselves often gets projected onto the world around us. The moments in my past when I wasn't very kind to others were connected to feelings of hate I had for myself, and in general, people who treat others with hostility and aggression are likely treating themselves with the same attitude.

Someone who truly loves herself will naturally extend this love to the people around her. Her words and actions will be compassionate and uplifting. When we love ourselves, we love others; and when we love others, we love ourselves. If you spread positivity, you will start to direct a certain amount of this positivity toward yourself—not to mention, you will also attract kindness and goodwill from other people.

Visualize Your Dreams

Even if we are not where we want to be in life, we usually know what will make us happy. We are all energy, and our minds are masters at creating and directing our reality.

Try to imagine the life you want to have and the person you want to be, in vivid detail. You will attract powerful energy and beautiful circumstances that will help you to reach those goals. For example, visualize who you would be if you were confident, even if you don't consider yourself a confident person at this moment. How would you act? What would you wear? What would you be doing? With whom would you be spending your time? How would you speak to yourself and others?

So many powerful people have spoken about the importance of visualizing the life you want, as if it were already here. Seeing is believing, so allow yourself to daydream about the life you're worthy of—and take steps toward changing your reality so that it matches your values.

Face Your Fears

Confronting our fears is one of the most powerful ways to move past our insecurities, and it's also one of the hardest. When we are insecure, we tend to be afraid of a lot of things. For example, if you're insecure about a part of your body, you probably spend a lot of time and energy hiding it from the world, to your great detriment. That fear of exposure reinforces your lack of confidence and allows you to remain small, so that you can feel some amount of control over your life. However, if you are never challenged to move beyond your comfort zone, you can never grow or evolve, or step into a full acceptance of who you are.

I suggest that if you feel insecure about some aspect of your body, instead of hiding it, wear something that shows it off—or take a photograph of that part and post it on social media.

I recall a time when I began to feel weird about revealing my face without makeup. I didn't wear it often, but because much of my art and social media content requires adornment, I became accustomed to wearing more and more...until I felt somewhat naked if I wasn't wearing any. To stop feeling that way, I took a professional photograph of my face without makeup. The photo highlighted all the fine lines, discoloration, pimples, and marks on my face. It felt uncomfortable to post the photo on Instagram, but after a while, I felt relief to reveal a side of me I wasn't accustomed to sharing on social media.

Doing things that make us uncomfortable at first is a powerful way to push our boundaries so that we can grow. You don't need to take a flying leap into your fears; step by step, you can gradually wade out into the unknown and develop greater courage. Once you are out of your comfort zone, life will truly begin to get more interesting and you'll notice yourself attracting the confidence, relationships, and situations you've always wanted.

Do the Things That Make You Feel Good

It is important to do things that make you feel happy and to stop doing things that minimize or erode your sense of worth. If a certain activity, relationship, professional path, or anything else brings you down, take steps to change your situation.

However, be willing to ask yourself if these aspects of your life are truly making you feel bad. Often, we get so accustomed to refusing joy that we might end up fearing good things because we are not used to letting in that kind of nourishment. But if you determine that something is really toxic, take action to distance yourself from it.

Fill your life with the things that interest you and make your heart sing: music, art, nature, knowledge, connections with people you love—the list goes on and on. Those things will help you maintain a positive state of mind, which can be extremely helpful in your journey of self-love. Be proactive in following your bliss. Learn new things, work on yourself, and be consistent in the work you need to do in order to reach your goals.

Stop Comparing Yourself to Others

Comparisons are something I have made a lot of in different areas of my life—with respect to not only my appearance but also to my life accomplishments and my perceived shortcomings. I've spent way too much time thinking of myself as "not enough" because I saw people younger than me whose achievements felt bigger than mine.

It's crucial to remember that each one of us has a unique path; comparing yourself to anyone else is as fruitless as a lion comparing itself to a whale. Life is full of beautiful diversity, and someone else's special qualities and accomplishments will never invalidate yours or diminish your shine. In the words of Judy Garland, "Be a first-rate version of yourself instead of a second-rate version of someone else." Bring your focus back to yourself and your journey of self-love, and things will come to you in good time.

There is nobody in the world who is exactly like you, so it makes sense that there is a unique path that exists especially for you. It has its own shape, rhythm, and timeline. You find your path and learn to walk it when you allow the universe to guide you and when you surrender the idea that your achievements need to resemble anyone else's. When you do this, you realize that what is meant for you will come to you at the perfect moment: when you are ready to receive it.

AFTERWORD

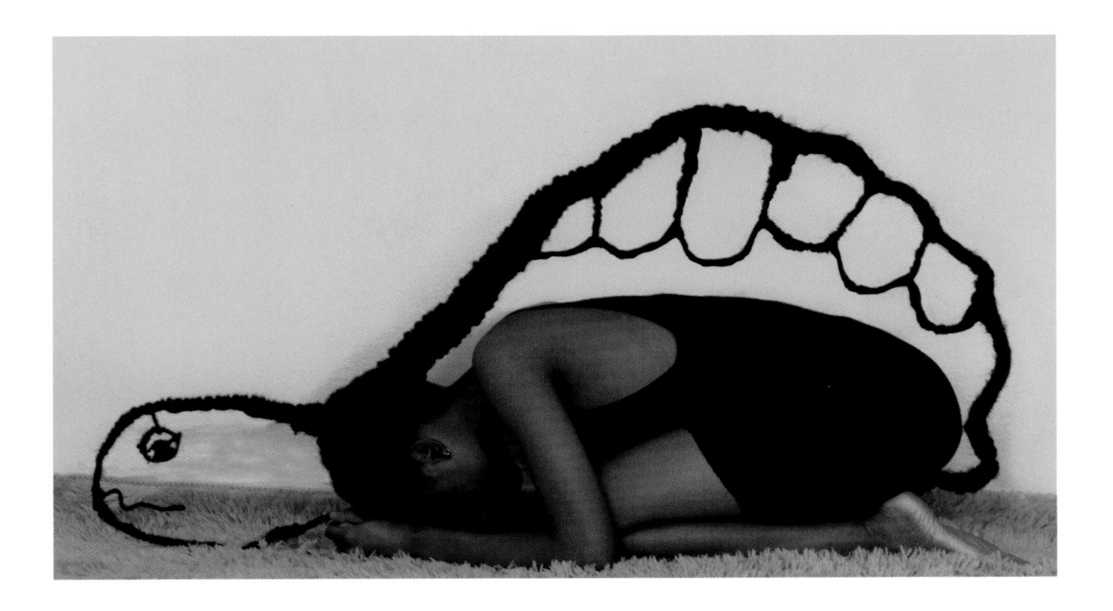

My life journey has been a remarkable one. I have learned a great deal about the power of resilience and faithfulness to my dreams, no matter what the world around me might be telling me. The effects have been amazing. In using my art as a way to love all aspects of myself—my origins, my colors, my body, my mind, my womanhood, my African identity, my overall self—I started to use the energy and positivity as fuel for dreaming big.

Every single one of us has an important story that only we have the capacity to tell. When we embrace this capacity as a responsibility to ourselves and the world around us, we develop the strength to fight for our dreams—even the ones that may seem totally impractical. Every day, I tell myself that I am unstoppable—and this mindset enables me to achieve greatness in even the seemingly small things, since I view every moment of my life as an opportunity to share who I am with honesty and integrity.

I started out like a turtle who hid in her shell and avoided interacting with the world. I didn't express my true self, because society told me it would not be accepted or appreciated. Today, I am a butterfly. I allow my beauty to be visible to all, and I let my curiosity be my guide. I remind myself that even if the world around me clings to its prejudices, my essence is transformative. Freedom is a journey that never ends—we must always move toward liberation and unlearn ways of being that keep us stuck in oppressive beliefs.

I acknowledge that the world around me is constantly transmitting harmful messages. This world never ceases to inform me that I cannot truly be free as a Black woman. However, I know this is a lie that all of us who are marginalized must work to shatter. The sky is not the limit, and when we learn to distinguish lies from the truth, we discover that we can soar.

As a Black woman, my journey has also been about learning to be my own best friend and advocate. I will never wait for someone else to fight for me and give me my freedom. I must take accountability for my own transformation. I must speak and express myself freely, as I am the only one who can claim my truth and share my beauty. I've always made the conscious choice to use myself as a canvas. Some might consider me, a dark-skinned Black woman, ugly compared to a light-skinned person. This is another lie: using my own body as art shows the world the beauty of dark skin.

I'm happy that I've changed the lives of some young women, and I hope this book will change the lives of even more. I want you, my reader, to see this book as a love letter that celebrates your own potential to change the world—to turn it into a beautiful canvas that reflects your own dreams and aspirations. May it give you the courage to hope for more, to find unexpected possibilities around each corner, and to settle for nothing less than a world that will embrace every single part of who you are. May this book give you the spark to believe in yourself and to be fearless in your self-expression, even if you live in a society in which the odds are stacked against you.

As women and citizens of the world, we are more than ready to join our voices together in one strong and unrelenting chorus. We are ready to challenge the status quo in every aspect of our lives: from the beauty industry to our governments to our own families. We are ready to claim our true worth and to let our light shine bright.

May you be a beacon of love and justice in your words, deeds, and actions. And remember that you are not alone.

Love,
Laetitia Ky

Acknowledgments

I would like thank all of those who worked on the book. First, to Nirmala Nataraj for helping me bring my words to life. To Lynn Grady, Sara Stemen, and the team at Princeton Architectural Press for believing in my work. Thanks to David Kuhn and Arlie Johansen, my book agents, and Carl Navarro at Elite World Group. And finally, thank you to my little sister, Florencia—without your support, none of this would have been possible.

Published by
Princeton Architectural Press
202 Warren Street
Hudson, New York 12534
www.papress.com

Printed and bound in China
25 24 23 22 4 3 2 1 First edition

Editor: Sara Stemen
Designer: Morcos Key

Credits
—
page 52:
Top left: Johannes Adolf Büchner, "Wangara woman (a muslim) in Sampa near Nwereme with typical hair decorations and remarkable hairstyle," Basel Mission Archives, D-30.62.025
Top right: Johannes Adolf Büchner, "Wangara woman (a muslim) in Sampa near Nwereme with typical hair decorations and remarkable hair-style," Basel Mission Archives, D-30.62.024
Bottom left: The National Library of Scotland
Bottom right: Special Collections, Yale Divinity School Library
—
page 55:
Top left: Special Collections, Yale Divinity School Library
Top right: © DM, Lausanne, Switzerland
Bottom: Rudolph Fisch, "Women dressing their hair," Basel Mission Archives, D-30.24.020

Library of Congress
Cataloging-in-Publication Data
—
Names: Ky, Laetitia, 1996- author.
Title: Love and justice : a journey of empowerment, activism, and embracing Black beauty / Laetitia Ky.
Description: First edition. | New York : Princeton Architectural Press, [2022] | Summary: "The personal story in words and photos of artist and activist Laetitia Ky, known for sculpting her own hair to create powerful and joyful artwork that embraces the beauty of Black hair and style, the fight for social justice, and the journey toward self-love" —Provided by publisher.
Identifiers: LCCN 2021029404 | ISBN 9781648960529 (hardcover)
Subjects: LCSH: Ornamental hairwork—Côte d'Ivoire. | Ky, Laetitia, 1996—Political and social views. | Women sculptors—Côte d'Ivoire—Biography. | Models (Persons)—Côte d'Ivoire—Biography. | Human rights workers—Côte d'Ivoire—Biography. | Women—Côte d'Ivoire—Social conditions. | Social problems in art.
Classification: LCC NK6076 .K93 2022 | DDC 709.2—dc23
LC record available at https://lccn.loc.gov/2021029404